W9-ASJ-367

DATE DUE

JAN 20 '96			

Women and Peace

SUNY Series, Global Conflict and Peace Education

Betty A. Reardon, Editor

Women and Peace

Feminist Visions of Global Security

Betty A. Reardon

State University of New York Press

Published by
State University of New York Press, Albany

For information, address State University of New York Press,
State University Plaza, Albany, N.Y. 12246

Production by M. R. Mulholland
Marketing by Fran Keneston

Library of Congress Cataloging-in-Publication Data

Reardon, Betty.
    Women and peace : feminist visions of global security / Betty A.
Reardon.
        p.   cm.—(SUNY series, global conflict and peace education)
    Includes bibliographical references (p.   ) and index.
    ISBN 0-7914-1399-3 (CH   :   acid-free).—ISBN 0-7914-1400-0 (PB   :
acid-free)
    1. Women and peace.   2. Feminism.   I. Title.   II. Series.
JX1965.R39   1993
327.1'72'082—dc20   92-9682
                                                                          CIP

10   9   8   7   6   5   4   3   2   1

Contents

Preface

Women and Peace: Feminist Visions of Global Security grew out of a study kit, "Women and Peace," published in 1989 as one of a series of "Women and Development Kits" produced by the Joint United Nations Information Committee (JUNIC) Non-Governmental Organization (NGO) Programme Group on Women at UN Headquarters in Geneva, Switzerland. The idea for the kit was originated by the UN Division for the Advancement of Women (DAW) and was issued by the division as Kit No. 5 from the United Nations Office in Vienna, Austria. I served as the substantive consultant for the project, gathering readings and drafting a core narrative to serve as a study guide. This book is substantially different from the kit, especially in organization and interpretation, and new material has been added and much left out from the original kit. Nonetheless, the kit was the starting point and core of this work.

As with most such collaborative projects, the final kit was the product of the efforts of many involved in JUNIC, the NGOs, and DAW. The original draft and readings were edited to accommodate UN guidelines and the diverse and divergent perspectives of the participants in the process. As the major editor on the project wrote me, "These kits are always a miracle of compromise between the diplomatic reticence of the U.N. system and the greater freedom of expression which the NGO's are fortunate enough to enjoy, although in this case there was considerable disagreement, too, among NGO's with regard to both peace activism and feminism." The latter no doubt is a reflection of the fact that, in her words, "any meeting on the subject of peace is bound to be difficult." And we can add, any discussion of feminist perspectives is bound to be controversial.

Indeed, the kit was a miracle of compromise, the very stuff of which peace itself is made. That miracle was in large measure due to the communicative capacity and editorial skills of Jeanne Vickers, who midwifed the miracle of "Women and Peace" as well as other study kits (a number of them are now available from DAW in Vienna). Much of what appears in this book is the result of her capacities and skills.

The portions of this book that are taken from the kit are primarily those that describe the conditions and circumstances surrounding women and peace. All of the analytic material that is not specifically attributed to another author is my own; and I alone am responsible for interpretations of the analytic and descriptive material.

Except for quotations from official United Nations documents, none of the material is endorsed by the United Nations, nor JUNIC, nor any NGO. I have, however, maintained the emphasis on the perspectives and contributions of the world organization because I believe that without the catalyst of the International Decade for Women, many of the significant advances in women's opportunities to participate in international affairs would not have been possible. Further and perhaps even more significant, the Forward Looking Strategies for the Advancement of Women, the ultimate policy product of the Decade for Women, I consider to be a blueprint for the socioeconomic policy changes essential to the emergence of a just world peace. Far too little attention is given to the contributions and the potential of the United Nations by peace researchers, feminist scholars, and activists, indeed, by the peace movement itself.

Feminism and peace advocacy, as I have argued elsewhere (*Sexism and the War System,* 1985), are grounded in similar purposes and values; and each has a reciprocal need of the other to achieve its purpose. While that premise is widely accepted, the degree and nature of that interdependence continue to be matters of controversy and differences among both feminists and peace advocates. This manuscript includes the perspectives of several feminists, but as I have noted, the interpretations are my own, the reflections of one feminist who speaks only for herself, but in the hope that other feminist perspectives will be brought to bear on the issues discussed here. This short book seeks to offer the conceptual definitions that have informed my own analysis, but it is in no way definitive. It is, as the title indicates, largely speculative and intends to be provocative, to promote discussion and further speculation, and to encourage more intensive study and research into the alternatives derived from speculative discussion.

This book is intended as the core of a wider inquiry into women and peace, as an impetus to further study of a rapidly developing field. It offers both questions for discussion and suggestions for further reading, as well as a bibliography on women and peace. The bibliography and the reading suggestions are limited. The fields of study and research related to the topics addressed here have produced significant bodies of literature. Feminist scholarship in particular offers much that has not been integrated into this discussion. I hope, however, that what is offered here will be instrumental in initiating further and more inclusive study of an issue still given too little attention in the discussions and analyses of the problems of peace and security. I hope this book will be useful in courses on women's studies, peace studies, global issues, and the United Nations. It is my hope that no matter what subject occasions its use, it will be a vehicle for consideration of the UN and the institutional and organizational needs of a world community committed to equality, development, and peace.

To Jeanne Vickers, whose career in international civil service has been followed by equally constructive service to the world society through the non-governmental community; to Dorota Giercyz, who vigorously pursues the possibilities for strengthening women's role in international affairs through the United Nations; to Edith Ballentyne of the Women's International League for Peace and Freedom, who helps to focus NGO attention on women's contributions to peace; to Diana Sheridan of the University of Oregon's Center for the Study of Women in Society, who like many feminist scholars focuses her work on women's reality and the practical applications of scholarship to social change; to Leslie Scott of the University of Oregon's Peace Studies Programs, who prodded me to do this book; Xujing Jia whose patience and typing skills produced the manuscript; to the millions of women all over the world who have carried on the struggle for authentic peace throughout their lifetimes, and in solidarity with the founding mothers of the women's peace movement and with the women on all sides of armed conflict, I express my admiration, my gratitude, and my sisterhood.

One

Introduction: A Decade for Difference

The full and effective promotion of women's rights can best occur in conditions of international peace and security.

— The Nairobi Forward Looking Strategies for the Advancement of Women, para. 13

Why Women and Peace?

For centuries the human family in all its forms and all its habitats has struggled to achieve security and live in peace. For most of human history, this struggle has been carried out by and on behalf of separate branches of the family, most of them unaware of the full variety and multiple lifestyles of the whole of humanity. The largest single component of the family to achieve peace and security for its own people has been the nation-state, a human grouping only a few centuries old. Even maintaining peace and security for all, within nations, has always been problematic, and, in our own time, an especially elusive goal, but maintaining peace among nations has been so problematic that it is a major public concern of our time. In 1945, at the close of the widest, most destructive war in human history, people of the independent nations of the world, in founding the United Nations, agreed that they must struggle together to "avoid the scourge of war" and create a just and lasting peace. As we move toward the close of the twentieth century, the fulfillment of that agreement is the most urgent task faced by the peoples of the Earth. The scourge still plagues the planet. Armed struggle within and between nations continues. Tension, hostility, and threat frequently characterize international relations and have incited nations to develop and produce ever more destructive and more numerous weapons. The human family seems to have gained the capacity to destroy itself but not to have learned how to live in peace, a peace that must now include the entire family in all its variety throughout the world.

During the closing decades of the twentieth century, we have experienced, perhaps for the first time, the full realization of the meaning of war and the possibilities for peace. We have seen both the decline of the cold war and the rise of the threat of regional, civil, and "low intensity" conflicts. We have witnessed a reaffirmation of the role of the United Nations in the pursuit and maintenance of peace, and recognized that the possibilities for peace relate inextricably to the future of the environment and the quality and speed of world development. We are, too, beginning to recognize that the struggle for fundamental human rights and freedom is more than the work of laying the foundation of peace. It is the articulation and realization of the very essence of peace. Above all, with the help of the field of peace research and many of the studies sponsored by the United Nations, we have come to recognize that the central problem of peace is violence, in all its forms, at all levels of society. We are, as well, coming to appreciate the complex and comprehensive nature of peace, that it is the sum of the interrelationships of a multiplicity of global problems. Most hopeful of our contemporary learnings is the dim but steadily brightening light of realization that all people are but one species, male and female are all one humanity.

The public awareness of these meanings, possibilities, and interrelationships has been in no small measure due to the second wave of the women's movement, which took on great momentum in the middle of this century and found its voice and visions most clearly and universally in the United Nations International Women's Decade 1975-85. The agenda set during that decade became the outline of a comprehensive "positive" peace and demonstrated that, in spite of great obstacles and limitations, the United Nations was the essential channel and institutional mechanism for the realization of the social aspirations of the human family.

It was women who formulated and propelled this agenda. It is women who continue to envision humane alternatives for world society. It is women whose resistance to war and struggle for social justice and human rights have in fact provided many of our concepts of positive peace, of the conditions of human society that permit all to live authentically human lives. From the ancient days of Lysistrata to those of Women for Mutual Security, women have believed in, demonstrated about, and struggled for "another way," for an attainable and viable alternative to war. Women's visions, their strivings, sufferings, and frustrations, are the very substance of the struggle for peace, a universal aspiration of multiple and varied character. Women's struggle has been against making differences among people a rationale for exclusion and oppression. As they have striven to be equal with men socially, economically, and politically, they have also called attention to the need to acknowledge the authentic, complementary differences between men and women. Indeed, they insist on honoring human differences of all kinds in the name of authentic human equality.

The United Nations International Women's Decade (UNDW), 1975–85), irrevocably changed the world's general acceptance of women's subservient status. Its positive focus on difference has had a profound impact on our present and for our future. Not only did the International Women's Decade create a climate for renewed criticism and change regarding the injustices suffered by women, it also firmly established the need for their full and equal participation in all human affairs, for the sake of justice for women and to guarantee the human family's survival. Also, the decade vigorously demonstrated the inseparable interrelationships among the goals embraced by the themes of the decade—equality, development, and peace—as well as the connections among the myriad global issues and problems that pose obstacles to the realization of these goals. Most significant of all, it brought to public attention a new way of looking at the world, an alternative view of public concerns and global issues. Women's views, heretofore given little or no attention in policy making, now are the subject of pollsters' surveys, and data classified by gender is more common. The views from the other half of humanity emerged as fresh, dynamic, integrated, and constructive perspectives on the world and the human condition. These views and women's problem-solving actions, many believe, offer the best hope for reducing armed conflict, preventing poverty, and preserving the Earth. In her film *Decade of Our Destiny*,[1] feminist researcher and filmmaker Bettina Corke depicts women from all areas of the world and in many fields of endeavor articulating their visions of women's roles in structuring the peaceful human community envisioned by the founders of the United Nations. Such argument has also been made by leading men[2] as well as women analysts of global issues, one of them a well-known African scholar.

> The fate of humanity may indeed depend upon relative communication and androgynization of the command structures. Those social movements which embrace contact and communications and those which seek to expand the role of women may turn out to be the most critical of all. (Mazrui 1986)

The International Women's Decade, by introducing women's issues as global issues, has also affected concepts of peace that have become broader and more complex, far beyond merely an absence of or period between wars. The possibilities for peace rest in large measure on the possibilities for women, for their full emancipation and for the realization of their visions of peace and security.

Defining and Assessing Peace:
A Set of Humane Global Conditions

There is no single, universal definition of peace. The concepts and experience of peacefulness are as varied as human cultures and perspectives. While there is a growing realization that peace is not simply the antithesis of war, peace activists agree that the reduction and elimination of war is a goal never to be abandoned until achieved. The abolition of the most devastating instruments of war, nuclear weapons and other weapons of mass destruction, must be achieved as soon as possible if we are to continue the struggle toward the achievement of a just, viable, and lasting peace. Most would also agree that peace will be lasting only to the degree that it is just, fair to all the Earth's peoples, and viable, acceptable to all nations and people. Such an ambitious goal might influence some to reject the possibility of peace as an unattainable ideal, were it not for the continuous, vigorous efforts of many to define and strive toward components of that goal. Peace is envisioned as a complex of specific political, economic, and social changes that make the world in some part more just and increase the areas of agreement among nations and peoples. It is a continuous process contributing to the viability of, and extending those elements of, peace we have attained. The daily work of peace is carried on by the United Nations, nongovernmental organizations, peoples' movements, and individual citizens. Millions throughout the world are engaged in the struggle for peace, and women are in the forefront of all these arenas. But still the question remains: What is peace?

A goal sought by so many, in such a disparate, far-flung, unstructured endeavor, as is the current struggle for peace, must of necessity be broad and comprehensive. While peace clearly means preventing such violence as armed conflict, military occupation, intervention by one country in the affairs of others, and, in general, reducing the role and threat of force in human affairs, it also means the "enjoyment of economic and social justice, equality, and the entire range of human rights and fundamental freedoms" (*The Nairobi Forward-Looking Strategies for the Advancement of Women*[3] 1985, paragraph 13; hereafter cited as "FLS"). Peace means as well a set of relationships among peoples and nations based on trust, cooperation, and recognition of the interdependence and importance of the common good and mutual interests of all peoples. In short, it is based upon the recognition that the Earth is a single, interdependent system, with one common future, and that all people belong to one species, have the same fundamental human needs, are endowed with full human dignity, are entitled to the full realization of all human rights, and share a common interest in the future of the Earth. Such a recognition calls upon those who would struggle for peace to work for a set of humane and equitable global social conditions that fulfill human needs, contain violence, and preserve the Earth. Much of the violence that afflicts human society results from a lack of equity. The poverty that prevents the meeting of basic human needs, the injustices and inequalities that constitute gross violation of human rights, are often at the root of international tension and distrust, the threat of force, and armed conflict. And armed conflict today, actual and potential, still threatens the very future of the planet.

To struggle for peace, then, is to endeavor to achieve such a set of humane and equitable global social conditions. It requires the conceptualization of, policy making for, and implementation of objectives and strategies for social development that are based upon the fulfillment of human needs and the health of the planet. The formulation and implementation of such objectives and policies require the full and equitable participation of those whose lives are to be affected by the policies. Rural development calls for the direct involvement of the rural peoples whose needs are to be fulfilled. Technical and industrial development calls for the involvement of both technical and industrial workers and potential consumers of the resulting products. These and most other forms of development call for the equal participation of women, who in many cases, as in the electronics production and agricultural sectors of the developing world, make up a significant portion of the work force.

To struggle for peace also is to insist upon the full and fair, universal enjoyment of human rights as set forth in the Universal Declaration of Human Rights and all of the covenants and conventions intended to protect and implement those rights. It is to endeavor to assure the application of these standards to all relevant situations, to hold governments responsible for the observation and application of the standards, and to hold individuals and governments accountable for their violation. To struggle for peace is also to recognize and strive not only for individual rights, but also for the collective rights of peoples, especially for the rights to a healthful environment and to "a

social and international order in which . . . rights and freedoms . . . can be fully realized" (Universal Declaration of Human
Rights, art. 28). Indeed, it might be argued that peace is a social
environment that favors the full development of the human person.
Such an environment is characterized, from local to global levels, by
tolerance, mutual respect, and serious endeavors to understand
differences, and to build community and confidence so that conflicts
can be resolved without recourse to violence. These characteristics in
turn depend upon equity and equality among nations, and ethnic
groups and between women and men, as recognized by the United
Nations Charter: "reaffirming faith in fundamental human rights, in
the dignity and worth of the human person, in the equal rights of men
and women and of nations, large and small" (Preamble, Charter of the
United Nations, 1945).

The connections and interdependence among issues of equity
and justice and war are reiterated in *The Nairobi Forward Looking
Strategies.* "The three objectives of the Decade . . . are broad,
interrelated and mutually reinforcing, so that the achievement of one
contributes to the achievement of another" (FLS, para. 9). In terms
of UNDW and FLS, equality refers not only to legal equality, the
elimination of discrimination by law, but also to equality of responsibility, and participation, and full recognition in social, economic,
and cultural life. While the International Women's Decade's documents emphasize equality between women and men, the basic concept of equality on which this emphasis is based is equality of all
persons and groups. The comprehensive notion of peace for which
equality is essential also requires the transcendence of the full range
of social and economic discrimination that impedes human development. Class and ethnic discrimination, age and/or religious discrimination, racism and apartheid, discriminatory international and
national economic structures that impede the development of the
poor nations—all of these inequalities must be transcended to achieve
a just and viable peace.

Development, the international code word for overcoming poverty
and attaining economic viability, is inextricably related to peace; it
should be a process that seeks to overcome such inequality and discrimination, particularly in the economic and social realms. In particular,
development for peace focuses on meeting human needs, including basic
physical needs and needs for the social, intellectual, aesthetic, and
spiritual development of the human person. And such development
would, as well, attend to the health of the natural environment in which
needs fulfillment is pursued. "Development also requires a moral

dimension to ensure that it is just and responsive to the needs and rights of the individual and that science and technology are applied within a social and economic framework that ensures environmental safety for all life forms on our planet" (FLS, para. 2).

Equality cannot be achieved without just development, and a viable peace is also impossible without these other two; "the full and effective promotion of women's rights can best occur in conditions of international peace and security" (FLS, para. 13).As women's equality can best be assured by international peace and security, so, too, development can be most effective under conditions of equality; and there can be little development without peace.

Women's movements for peace seek to demonstrate the connections among these issues and problems. Striving to understand these interrelationships is a major part of the struggles to achieve the humane conditions of a world guided by the standards of the Universal Declaration of Human Rights, the Forward Looking Strategies, and other standards set forth by the United Nations in its mission to achieve and maintain world peace.

The United Nations Framework for
Linking Women's Concerns with Peace

In the five decades of its history, the United Nations has been a major agent in addressing the day-to-day problems that lead to war and violence. Although decades of refusal and/or reluctance of member states to fulfill the peacekeeping function led many to believe the UN incapable of keeping the peace, its activities in making peace, programs and actions to reduce the violence of poverty and oppression, to advance development and human rights, have made the world organization essential to the world community. Most of this work, including that which has addressed women's issues, has been carried out by the specialized agencies, staffed by an international civil service committed to the welfare of the world community, not to the interests of one state or block of member states. The General Assembly (the representative chamber) and the Security Council (the seventeen-member body that addresses serious threats to peace) are the scenes of political differences and contending interests so often played up by the media. Both bodies, however, put forth recommendations that lead to constructive action by the agencies established under the Economic and Social Council.

The General Assembly has also adopted the declarations and conventions that have provided the standards of human rights, the main indicators of a peaceful and just world society, and the inspiration of movements to transcend all forms of violence. The Charter of the United Nations presupposed that "the scourge of war" could be avoided only if the dignity and worth of the human person, including equal rights of men and women, could be affirmed, international law maintained, and social progress and better living standards promoted. The authors of the charter believed that war arose from the absence of these conditions.[4]

The values of world peace and human dignity underlie all the work of the United Nations. Thus, the pursuit of peace has been an integral part of the global effort for the advancement of women, and the advancement of women has been pursued as integral and essential to peace. Each of the three United Nations world conferences held during the International Women's Decade (Mexico City, Mexico, 1975; Copenhagen, Denmark, 1980; and Nairobi, Kenya, 1985) dealt with the issue of peace in relation to the advancement of women.

The Mexico City conference in 1975 adopted the World Plan of Action for the Implementation of the Objectives of the International Women's Year. (The original effort was to be one year, but the dimensions of the task called for a decade.) The plan called "for the full participation of women in all efforts to promote and maintain peace."

The 1980 World Conference of the United Nations Decade for Women: Equality, Development, and Peace, in Copenhagen, concluded that progress toward any of the three main objectives has a beneficial effect on the others, and consequently that it is only under conditions of peace that it is possible to move forward to the full implementation of the other two objectives of the decade.

The 1985 World Conference to Review and Appraise the Achievements of the United Nations Decade for Women: Equality, Development, and Peace was convened at Nairobi. It adopted by consensus *The Nairobi Forward Looking Strategies for the Advancement of Women*, a significant set of standards for women's emancipation as fundamental to a peaceful society.

To integrate the views and concerns of ordinary citizens into these conferences, nongovernmental organizations (NGO's) held a forum at each of them, and at each of these forums, peace was a theme. The highlight of all these efforts came in Nairobi. The International Women's Forum the NGO's organized there included as one of its most energetic and colorful components a "Peace Tent," where women from all over the world exchanged ideas on peace issues and set in motion ways of collaborating and striving for peace that still have profound influences on women's peace movements.

Organizers and participants alike described the Peace Tent as one of the best used and most helpful aspects of the Forum. About half the day official programmes and dialogues were scheduled for the space and the other half was intentionally left available for women to disucss disputes which resulted from other programmes, either NGO or U.N. Organized by Feminists International for Peace and Food, this space allowed an alternative to the regular offerings and the traditional structure of problem-solving. Some governments saw this women's initiative as a threat to their own proceedings as all different nationalities were conversing in private about what they were not supposed to address in public, officially . . .

The spirit of the Peace Tent extended beyond the bounds of the physical space, as many participants voiced the need to start making connections between the issues they had identified throughout the Decade (Weigel 1990).

Apart from the Forward Looking Strategies, three other international legal instruments relating to women and peace have emerged from the United Nations system: an international convention to eliminate discrimination against women, a declaration on women's participation in the promotion of peace, and a declaration on the protection of women and children in war.

The United Nations Convention on the Elimination of All Forms of Discrimination against Women[5] was adopted by the General Assembly in 1979 and is the most comprehensive legal document on the advancement of women. The Preamble points out that many factors will contribute to the full attainment of the objectives of the International Women's Decade, and that both peace and development require the maximum participation of women on equal terms with men in all fields of life. A major instrument in the field of human rights protection, the convention clearly calls for the full and equal participation of women in civil and political affairs.

By April 1991, 104 states had ratified or acceded to the convention, among them four permanent members of the Security Council.[6] They agreed

to take all appropriate measures to eliminate discrimination against women in the political and public life of the country and, in particular, shall ensure to women, on equal terms with men, the right: (a) to vote in all elections and public referenda and to be eligible for election to all publicly elected bodies; (b) to participate in the formulation of government policy and the implementation thereof and to hold public office and perform all public functions at all levels of government; and (c) to participate in non-governmental organizations and associations concerned with the public and political life of the country. (United Nations Convention on the Elimination of All Forms of Discrimination against Women, art. 7)

The United Nations Declaration on the Participation of Women in Promoting International Peace and Cooperation makes it evident that the UN considers women's civil and political participation essential to peace. A specific statement on peace is found in this declaration, proclaimed by the General Assembly in 1982. Like all declarations, it is a standard-setting instrument with moral force, but not legally binding on member states. Nevertheless, it identifies the following crucial issues:

- Qualitative and quantitative increase in women's participation in the sphere of international relations
- Rendering solidarity and support to women victims of violations of human rights, particularly those identified as violations of group or "solidarity" rights, e.g., apartheid, racial discrimination, colonialism, foreign occupation
- Encouragement of women's participation in nongovernmental and intergovernmental organizations aimed at the strengthening of international peace and security
- Provision of practical opportunities for the effective participation of women and, to that end, equitable representation of women in governmental and nongovernmental functions, including in the secretariats of the United Nations system, in diplomatic service, and on delegations to national, regional or international meetings.

Clearly, these are goals still a long way from satisfactory achievement. Nonetheless, the international community has declared them to be necessary to the achievement of peace and security in the world. Women's political action groups have also adopted them as fundamental objectives for mobilizing other women across the globe.

The United Nations Declaration on the Protection of Women and Children in Emergency and Armed Conflict was proclaimed by the UN General Assembly in 1974 because of the effects of armed conflict on women and children. It called for strict observance by all member states. It, too, is not enforceable, but it sets a standard to be pursued in the struggle to overcome the sufferings of women and children and of all civilian populations affected by periods of emergency and war.

At a global level, responsibility for the implementation of the strategies, the convention, and the declarations rests with organizations of the United Nations system and their secretariats. The most directly relevant programs for women and peace are those of the United Nations Secretariat, especially the Division for the Advancement of Women in Vienna.

The Division for the Advancement of Women prepares in-depth reports on various aspects of women and peace issues for review by the Commission on the Status of Women. It also serves as the secretariat of the United Nations Committee on the Elimination of Discrimination against Women (CEDAW), which was set up to consider the progress made in implementation of the convention.

Many of the specialized agencies of the United Nations system also pursue activities relevant to women and peace. UNESCO has conducted a number of such activities, including an expert group meeting on the role of women in educating young people for peace, mutual understanding, and respect for human rights (1981) and an international seminar in 1986 on the development of a framework for women to participate in, and influence decisions related to, peace and justice and to promote international understanding for peace and development. Other UNESCO activities focus on the eradication of violence against women within the family and society, including studies on the sociocultural causes of prostitution, a practice based upon the sexual exploitation of both women and children.

The United Nations Commission on the Status of Women designated priority themes on women and peace for 1988–92. This commission is the intergovernmental body responsible for the implementation of the Nairobi Forward Looking Strategies. Consisting of forty-five member states, it meets annually to debate the priority themes for each of the goals of the strategies. It also has a mandate to include regular monitoring and review and appraisal of their implementation, and has devised a system to carry out this function at international and national levels. For the period 1988–92, in the area of peace, its themes were these:

- Access to information, education for peace, and efforts to eradicate violence against women within the family and society
- Full participation of women in the construction of their countries and in the creation of just social and political systems

- Women in areas affected by armed conflicts, foreign intervention, alien and colonial domination, foreign occupation, and threats to peace
- Refugee and displaced women and children
- Equal participation in all efforts to promote international cooperation, peace, and disarmament

The commission provides policy guidance to member states and to the United Nations system in order to achieve the full implementation of the Foward Looking Strategies regarding women and peace by the year 2000. To support this work, the United Nations is working on research and policy analysis.

Current research on the participation of women in decision-making processes related to peace and disarmament at national, regional, and world levels has several objectives: to present the situation of women in concrete, measurable terms on the basis of reliable data, to conduct thorough analyses leading to identification of obstacles, and to make recommendations for overcoming them. Much of this research is conducted in the form of case studies, such as a case study on decision making related to peace and disarmament in Sweden and, at the regional level, two case studies, namely, "Participation of Women in the Talks on Mutual Reduction of Armed Forces and Armaments and Associated Measures in Central Europe" and the "Vienna Meeting in 1986 of Representatives of the Participating States of the Conference on Security and Cooperation."[7]

The role of women in education for peace is another key area toward which the UN Branch for the Advancement of Women has directed its attention. One study interprets education for peace as a lifelong process that should take place worldwide in every situation, in every structure and process through which people and societies learn and conduct their private and public affairs. It is based on the assumption that women should participate fully in this process. They should do so as both contributors and beneficiaries, with equal access to information, education, and political participation. Such participation, the study asserts, would also benefit educational, political, and social processes and, consequently, society generally.

Thus, the objective of such research is to identify the obstacles to women's participation in education for peace, to encourage and promote coordination and research among various agencies, and to suggest concrete recommendations to governmental, nongovernmental, and intergovernmental organizations, including the United Nations system. An area in which study is still very much needed is that of women's unique and extensive contributions to peace education, its development and implementation.

A third priority area of the commission is the effect of conflict in society on women, particularly as expressed in various forms of violence against women. The interconnections between violence in the family, in society, and at the international level are only beginning to be explored. Indeed, violence in the family was finally diagnosed as a major social problem during the United Nations Decade for Women, mainly as a result of the efforts of the nongovernmental community, and the women's organizations that were among its main energizing forces.

A UN expert group meeting on the subject held in December 1986 explored many dimensions of the problem of violence in the family. Of particular concern is the *interrelation* between violence and inequality in society and within the family, including such difficult subjects as rape, involuntary prostitution, and sexual harassment, which are reflections of societal violence particularly directed toward women.[8] These links between domestic and social violence are one of the main reasons for women's special stake in peace.

Women's Stake in World Peace: A Feminist Perspective

The selection of peace as one of the three main themes of the United Nations Decade for Women resulted from the long tradition of women's concerns about the human suffering and devastating waste of resources exacted by war. It also reflected women's growing consciousness of their roles as supporters of the war system, as particular victims of war and all forms of peacelessness, and of the potential contribution they can make to world peace. Most of all, it manifests a significant increase in women's actions to affect policy making on issues of peace and security.

Women in their roles as homemakers, mothers, and caregivers have endured great hardships in wartime. Many must see their children, the aged, and the weak suffer deprivation when food supplies and other necessities are destroyed or sent to the war zones. Many have lost their homes. They have themselves, as have those they care for, fallen victim to armed attack. Through centuries of warfare, women have been left to tend to crops and children with none to defend them should their lands be invaded. In societies where women's status and welfare depends almost entirely on their relationship to men, widows are often left without means to provide for themselves and their children. Thus, to the immediate pain of the loss of husbands, fathers, sons, and brothers is added the longer—term suffering of further deprivation.

Women, too, as has been well documented in recent research on development and arms spending, bear the greatest burden of the world's poverty and suffer the lack of very fundamental needs and amenities, which might be more adequately provided were not so large a portion of the world's resources spent on war and the preparation for war.[9]

While these circumstances fall especially hard on women and children, men too suffer the same "disasters of war" both in and outside the military. We need only think of the aged male faces seen among the photographs of bomb victims and refugee camps. Both men and women are victims of warfare and peacelessness, and both contribute to the lack of peace. Granted, relatively few women actively fight in wars, and even fewer participate in the decisions to wage war or in making the policies that place military strength above human needs; however, without the contributions of women to the building and maintaining of warmaking capacities, war could not be waged. Women have supported their nations' military efforts in times of war. In World War II, for example, some women served in noncombat roles in the armed forces, and thousands served in other support capacities—for instance, as workers in the factories that supplied the instruments of war. Today, many work in plants that produce parts for the most destructive weapons ever devised. In time of war, women maintain "the homefront," care for the wounded, keep the economy running, and give their sons and husbands to the fighting forces. Indeed, many are proud to be the "gold star mothers" or war widows of fallen soldiers. Most women raise their sons to be ready to serve their nations in time of armed conflict and, while not without pain and reluctance, "wave them off to war." And now some raise their daughters for such service, too.

what about the women who choose to be part of their country's political and military conflicts? What about the growing numbers of women, including mothers, serving in the United States military since 1973, for example? The National Organization for Women (NOW) has ended by supporting the move for women to be eligible for combat on the perfectly rational ground of professional opportunity equity: Congresswoman Pat Schroeder has written a bill to adopt a Pentagon group's suggestions that the Army test women in combat roles; and syndicated columnist Ellen Goodman has come down on the side of women in combat, arguing that "any war that isn't worth a woman's life isn't worth a man's life." As I write, the television news is filled with the voices of eager young American women serving in Saudi Arabia pleading for the privilege of combat duty. (Forcey 1990, p3)

"Desert Storm" did offer them that privilege. Although women served in field support service and not technically in combat, five American military women were killed in action in the Gulf War, and one was taken prisoner. Perhaps because the public accepted this, the Schroeder bill was adopted in May 1991, lifting previous restrictions, and this just days before we saw the Mother's Day return of many young women embracing toddlers and infants after months in the Middle East.

So, too, women are participants in the structures of discrimination and deprivation often cited as a major obstacle to a just and viable peace in the world. In the capitalist industrial countries, women as well as man are the beneficiaries of a world economic system that discriminates against the poor nations of the world. In many countries, some women have far easier lives and more personal freedoms because other women are forced by economic circumstances to do household work and child care outside their own homes. Such workers are frequently women of color working in Caucasian homes, a reflection of further inequities imposed on the basis of color. Thus in the United States and various other countries, some women bear the triple burdens of economic, sexual, and racial discrimination.

Women are in no way divorced from the structures of inequity, poverty, and oppression, nor are they totally without responsibility for the continuation of the institution of war. While some argue that the mothering experience predisposes women to favor peace (Ruddick 1989), they are not predisposed by their hormonal balance to pacifism, any more than men are predisposed to warmongering. It is rather the social roles women have played through history that have led many to feel the burden of war, and value the opportunities of peace, more openly and avidly than most men.

Human beings tend to place a high value on that in which they invest their care and effort, they manifest concern for what they are responsible for. I tend to believe that it could well be this factor that induces male policy makers to give priority to industrial and military production. Whereas testosterone probably does account for greater aggressivity in males than in females, there is no law of nature that determines that such aggressivity need be violent or destructive. As I have argued elsewhere (Reardon 1985), the differences in attitude and perspectives between women and men are learned and derive not from biology but from society.

Society has assigned to men responsibility for the production, maintenance, and defense of its infrastructure. Women produce and nurture human life, well-being, and relationships. All of us tend to defend as vigorously as we can that which we consider to be our life's work. "I Didn't Raise My Boy to Be a, Soldier," the title of a women's peace movement song of World War I, is doubly misleading—not only because, as we have noted, most women do raise their sons to serve their societies, including military service; but also because it is not the soldiering, but its consequences, they abhor. Women do not raise children to be killed or to kill the children of others; to serve, yes, to destroy and be destroyed, no.

So it is as vigorous contributors to its promotion and maintenance that women's stake in world peace has become so widely recognized. Women in all nations, from all sectors of society, are vocal and active advocates of international understanding and peace, of the pursuit of disarmament and economic conversion, of trust building among nations, of negotiation of international differences and conflicts. Many tend to recognize their common and universal roles as caregivers, mothers, and nurturers. As *The War with Two Voices* (Deonna 1989) so poignantly illustrates, they find it harder to look upon each other as enemies, no matter what national differences divide them. Women's bearing and breastfeeding of infants, the biological function upon which the continuation of the human species depends, is seriously endangered by all warfare and certainly is being impaired by preparation for, and the consequences of, wars. It may be forever impaired by nuclear warfare. War-induced famines have desiccated the breasts of African women. Nuclear testing has deformed and aborted the babies of Pacific women. Many women throughout the world have come to see in this function of giving life and maintaining the species a special responsibility to struggle against that which, in damaging their own health and reproductive capacity, threatens the continuation of life and reduces its quality—weapons of mass destruction, warfare, poverty, and ecological devastation. But motherhood alone could hardly explain woman's fierce defense of peace, which involves many women who never have been, nor intend to be, mothers. More significant, I would argue, is the meaning and value of the work that fills their days. It is the work of building, growing, serving, nursing, teaching, weaving, cooking, cleaning, filing, typing, managing, administering; in short, the functions of developing and maintaining the living elements of human society. For women, security lies in making these functions possible.

More and more women acknowledge the linkage between peace, equality, and development as they become politically aware and active. While society has not placed adequate value on women's work, women know that without it society would not survive. The destruction of societies by warfare is in large part the destruction of women's daily labors. Women's activities in defense of peace are at base a defense of the fruits of their lives and labors as well as of the future of the human family. In small groups, in local communities, in large national organizations, and in international movements, women in larger and larger numbers have been, and are becoming vigorous, effective, and untiring promoters of world peace and defenders of society and the civil order that maintains them.

The connections among peace, equality, and development are acknowledged by more and more women, who in ever larger numbers are becoming politically aware and active, effective and untiring promoters of world peace. They link their demands for peace with very concrete social demands, with demands for development and for the solution of global problems. These demands derive from women's perspectives on the world, perspectives emerging from the most recent global circumstances to the most ancient local traditions.

While it is clear that women's traditional roles and social experience lead them to a special appreciation of peace, this alone does not account for their stake in it. More recent scholarship on women and peace, in exploring the links between sexism and militarism, has placed the question squarely in the domain of power and the political structures from which women are excluded (French 1985; Elshtain 1984; Stiehm 1983). When we move the discussion from women's experiences to feminist perspectives, we need to address the issues of power and inequitable political structures, and from this we take our definition of the term feminist. A feminist perspective or approach confronts the social, economic, and psychological reasons for this inequity, in order to rectify it. A feminist perspective seeks fundamental political change. A feminist perspective looks toward political possibilities for women beyond their traditional roles. This book is as much about how women are pursuing those possibilities as why they should pursue them. While it does not deal at length with the literature of the field, it is meant to be associated with the growing feminist scholarship on women and peace described below. (Much of this literature is listed in appendix 5.) It embraces Leslie Cagan's definition quoted by Colleen Roach.

> Defining feminism is no easy task. Leslie Cagan, an American feminist and social activist, offers a definition that is to my liking: "Feminism is a political perspective that demands an end

to the oppression of people because of their gender, and an end
to the institutional and individual structures that define men as
more valuable than women. Feminism rests on a belief that we
can live in a world without hierarchies of control and domination,
that people can exercise control over their own lives and live in
harmony with others, and that women can share equality of
opportunity and freedom" (Cagan, 1983, p. 94).

There are two sorts of feminist literature that are of relevance to
war, peace and culture. First of all, there is a very interesting
body of work by feminist peace researchers whose writings are
directly linked to the study of war and peace. Some of the names
that come to mind are Elise Boulding (Boulding, 1987, 1988a,
1988b), Betty Reardon (Reardon, 1985), Riane Eisler (Eisler,
1987), and Birgit Brock-Utne (Brock-Utne, 1985); there are
many others who have written on women and peace, such as
Leslie Cagan and Barbara Ehrenreich . . .

Many feminist peace researchers have incorporated both 'hard'
and 'soft' issues into their work: there is a real concern, for
example, in the writings of Elise Boulding and Betty Reardon
with the political economy of oppression and the effects of
militarism in the Third World. Yet they are not afraid also to talk
about the need for 'imaging' and 'imagining' new strategies for
peace, and relying more on the intuitive and nurturing sides of
human nature to build a new peace process.

Secondly, there is a body of feminist literature not directly
related to peace but which has been used by women peace
researchers because of its relevance to their work. Here, I am
referring, for example, to the work of Carol Gilligan, the Harvard
educator, whose book *In A Different Voice* (Gilligan, 1982)
became a touchstone for many peace researchers who have
argued that the different moral development of women make
them more prone to peace than men. (Roach 1991, p.3)

Women's Perspectives on Peace:
Feminist Possibilities for Human Security

Women's perspectives on peace are as rich and varied as are their
experiences, as professionals, farmers, soldiers, scientists, factory
workers, clerks, artists, astronauts, technicians, truck drivers, ciga-
rette makers, artisans, and in every other human occupation, includ-

ing homemakers. While women throughout the world share common responsibilities for families and households, the ways in which they fulfill these responsibilities are, in their diversity, a wonderful panoply of human possibilities. Yet there are, in their varied ways of meeting human needs and their multiple views of peace, universal strands that unite, as do their traditional roles in family and household, roles in which they seek to provide for the security of their families and communities. Worldwide, women have come to see their own liberation and full equality as essential to human security. Women's views of peace in the context of human security are articulated in *The Nairobi Forward Looking Strategies*; in articulating peace as that comprehensive set of global conditions previously described, the document speaks to the global aspirations of women everywhere when it states:

> The full and effective promotion of women's rights can best occur in conditions of international peace and security where relations among States are based on the respect for the legitimate rights of all nations, great and small, and peoples to self-determination, independence, sovereignty, territorial integrity and the right to live in peace . . .

> Peace includes not only the absence of war, violence, and hostilities at the national and international levels but also the enjoyment of economic and social justice, equality, and the entire range of human rights and fundamental freedoms within society.

> It also embraces the whole range of actions reflected in concerns for security and implicit assumptions of trust between nations, social groups, and individuals. It represents goodwill toward others and promotes respect for life while protecting freedom, human rights, and the dignity of peoples and of individuals. Peace cannot be realized under conditions of economic and sexual inequality, denial of basic human rights and fundamental freedoms, deliberate exploitation of large sectors of the population, unequal development of countries, and exploitative economic relations. Without peace and stability there can be no development. Peace and development are interrelated and mutually reinforcing . . .

> Peace is promoted by equality of the sexes, economic equality, and the universal enjoyment of basic human rights and fundamental freedoms. Its enjoyment by all requires that women be

enabled to exercise their right to participate on an equal footing
with men in all spheres of the political, economic, and social life
of their respective countries, particularly in the decision-making
process, while exercising their right to freedom of opinion,
expression, information and association in the promotion of
international peace and cooperation. (FLS, para. 13)

These few paragraphs encapsulate many women's views of peace
and elucidate women's definitions of authentic, comprehensive global
security, the concept of global security that informs and provides the
framework for this book. That framework is referred to as "feminist"
because it derives from feminist analysis of women's approaches to
peace and from the work of feminist peace researchers who are
attempting to define security in more constructive and comprehensive
terms.   Maria Stern, one such feminist researcher, offers these
defining observations.

If one can gain inspiration and an alternative perspective from
the distinction between negative and positive peace, one can also
begin to view the concept of security in a novel way. By assigning
negative and positive values to the concept of security, one
develops a useful tool for analyzing different interpretations of
what it means to be secure. In the same sense, one gains insight
about the different subjective natures of peace. Negative peace and
negative security rely on a desire to inhibit the existence of a
destructive entity, while positive peace and positive security rest
on a desire to create a constructive entity . . .

The concept of negative security stems from the conventional
"power politics" paradigm and rests on the premise of deterrence.
This means that security results from the cancellation of one
threat by another or the protection from one threat by another;
security becomes the sum of two negative threats, and can
therefore be referred to as "negative" security. A simple and
everyday example of the logic behind negative security can be
found in the purchase of a household gun for self-protection from
crime. By having the means of threatening someone else, one
feels more safe, more secure.

Negative security implies a meeting or a countering of the actual
threat with an equally threatening device or perhaps an even
more threatening one. Thus, its objective involves the cancelling
out of one threat with another equally or more potent threat.

Therefore, the vision of a secure state, according to the logic of negative security, is a state which has the means to counter any military threat it may face—a state with a high level of military defense . . .

The positive notion of security, on the other hand, attempts to eliminate threat (military or other) by addressing its cause—such as the existence of nuclear weapons—as well as the threat itself. It does not advocate the countering of the actual threat with an additional threat. Positive security thus has a positive value instead of a negative one. It implies that the source of threat disappears, and is not merely countered, that one administers a cure for the disease, not simply the symptoms.(Stern 1991, pp 26-28)

Feminist security approaches seek to overcome and transform threats to the peace with positive conditions of mutual security. This thrust toward mutual security for all the world's people is typical of most women's actions for peace. These actions and views that are the base for feminist perspectives on security are inspired by women's work and experience.

Women's traditional roles of engaging in multiple activities, as generalists, have given them this broad, integrated view of peace and security that provides a hopeful alternative to the more narrow and fragmented views that most influence present processes of national and international security policy formation. Perhaps nothing can be more provocative of new ways of thinking about security than turning the present notions upside down. The shortest, strongest, and perhaps most meaningful way of describing this view is reversing the common relationship between means and ends. Women, as is evident from the foregoing passages quoted from *The Nairobi Forward Looking Strategies*, see peace as the route to security rather than the other way around. Gandhi's assertion, "There is no way to peace. Peace is the way," is an excellent summary of a feminine view of security, a view largely formed by women's experience of nurturing, caregiving, and household maintenance. Peace, as will be noted in the discussion of positive peace in chapter 3, provides the conditions and resources most conductive to caregiving and nurturing. War and preparation for war reduce and destroy resources and limit and complicate the conditions for care and nurture. Women who bring forth human life, and carry the responsibility for maintaining it and providing it with the most humane quality possible, see security in terms of the possibilities for life, its maintenance, and the improvement of its quality. Security lies in things hoped for and planned for, perhaps more than in things as they are. Security is in large part *futures perception*.

> Security, we argue, is as much a matter of perception as "reality"; as is well attested by the real insecurity produced by the present security system which (in spite of the warming of the Cold War) still relies heavily on armed force and the threat system, a reliance which erodes all other dimensions of security. Authentic human security, we believe, derives mainly from the reasonable expectation of well being. In that women's lives have been largely devoted to fulfilling expectations of well-being, feminists who see the relevance and values of women's experience discern it in a new multi-dimensional approach to security . . .

> The holistic feminist approach contrasts starkly with conventional security, views and policies which reduce virtually all the issues to the questions of "national security" and "military preparedness." The dysfunctionality of this reductionist view of security is readily evident to all who are concerned with the quality of the life to be made secure. Feminists see in its deleterious effects on women how the inordinate priority given to the military erodes authentic security, global, national, and local. (Scott and Reardon 1991)

What women householders and caregivers experience as authentic security is the expectation of well-being for those for whom they are providing care: their families, their communities, and the vulnerable and impoverished whose need for care and nurturance many women feel as they feel the needs of "their own." It is the pursuit of these positive expectations that women bring to the endeavor, both in the private sphere and in the public sphere, where they campaign for security at all social levels from neighborhood or village to the international system. Their campaigns reveal their notions of what constitutes security. Women's views of global security might be summarized as a world in which all the Earth's peoples could live with four fundamental expectations. And women's actions for peace are inspired by the severe threats to the realization of those expectations posed by the present world order.

First, that *our planet will continue to be able to sustain life*. Yet scientists have warned that the ozone layer has been so seriously damaged that it may be irreparable. The damage is causing severe harm to the human immune system and bringing about a drastic increase in skin cancer. Deforestation, especially in the Amazon Basin, has significantly reduced the Earth's supply of oxygen. Without sufficient oxygen, life cannot be sustained. Waters polluted by poverty and industrial misuse, and atmosphere damaged by weapons testing, are destroying natural systems. Yet research and development of chemical and biological weapons continue. The very weapons we have developed to defend our security are themselves a threat to our security in the potential consequences of their use in combat and in the actual processes of their development and testing.

Next, that *the basic needs of life will be met.* Yet, as more people of the world fall into poverty, millions are without clean, potable water, housing, adequate food, fundamental education, and health care of any kind. Most of these are women. Inflation is rampant, unemployment is increasing; uncared for children roam the streets of the world's great cities.

Third, that *human dignity and integrity will be respected, and personal well-being and possibilities for individual and social development will not be impeded by traditional customs, social structures, or political policies* at local, national, or global levels. Yet a review of the Declaration of the Convention on All Forms of Discrimination against Women provides a list of a broad and tragic range of impediments to women's personal well-being that still prevail throughout the world. Apartheid and racism in various forms impede the social development of many indigenous peoples. The arms produced for national defense have been used to maintain racist, repressive systems that deny the personal well being and human rights of ethnic groups and political dissenters.

Fourth, *that we can be protected from preventable harm* and cared for in times of disaster without enduring greater harm, that *the life and well-being of the Earth's peoples will not be harmed as a consequence of imbalanced security policies, preparation for war, and armed conflict.* Yet, in a highly militarized world, local conflicts rage that daily impose death and suffering on noncombatants as well as armed forces. The 1991 war in the Persian Gulf and the 1992 war in a disintegrating Yugoslavia took uncounted numbers of civilian lives, produced hundreds of thousands of refugees, and reduced living conditions to circumstances that of themselves were lethal. A flourishing trade in conventional arms fuels the flames of these conflicts and consumes resources in a truly incendiary manner, leaving in ashes people's hopes for even a minimal standard of life. The technological arms race, with its advancing weapons development, has also further diverted resources from social and human purposes as it escalates to the point of the possibility of total destruction. Arms development cannot be relied upon to prevent aggression and warfare. A case can be made that, on the contrary, arms production and trafficking encourage armed conflict, eroding rather than assuring our expectation of protection or "defense."

Each of these expectations has been the focus of major United Nations reports and declarations on development, human rights, the environment, and disarmament and security. But little public heed has been paid. However, women's movements and initiatives are insisting that we must turn our attention to meeting these four fundamental expectations that constitute authentic security. They help to point out that we must attend to the obstacles to these expectations in an integrated, comprehensive fashion based on an understanding of the interrelationships among them. Until we understand the connections among these four expectations and the other global problems deriving from their frustration, neither the world nor any of its people will be secure. Alternative approaches are an urgent necessity. Women's experiences and feminine values are sources of such alternatives.

Feminine Characteristics as Approaches to Peace and Security

The discussions in this book and elsewhere of the need for women's participation in public affairs are essentially a call to valorize those feminine characteristics that are conducive to peace and comprehensive approaches to security. Some feminists argue that these characteristics hold the greatest possibilities to move us from the present condition of continuous armed conflict, potential nuclear annihilation, and ecological collapse toward the achievement of a truly just world peace and authentic global security.

Both men and women feminists have asserted that women's approaches to social relations and economic necessity reflect desperately needed capacities that all human beings could develop, capacities that could drastically improve the chances for the survival of human society. Many believe that in women's experiences and skills as nurturers there are possibilities for unprecedented policies to sustain the Earth and support her peoples. Millennia of strict role separation, women in the private realm of the home and men in the public realm of the political economy, have produced within the private realm modes of accommodating differences and mediating conflict that not only preserve relationships but also contribute to the health and development of the group. Women's roles within the family have produced a repertoire of skills continuously and effectively applied in the domestic sphere but ignored or rejected in the public sphere. These skills and the values that underlie them, feminists argue, may well be the tools for the construction of a more secure and humane world order. In themselves, they are reasons for including women on an equal basis with men in the discourse defining security and the process of making public policy.

Women's exercise of the value of care can teach us to find the ways to transform our economic structures so as to make them capable of meeting human needs. The feminine concern with relationship can show us how to maintain the web of global interdependence, to find the grounds for common efforts among all peoples toward the achievement of mutual security, even and especially for those in conflict. Women's practiced need to create constructive compromises could help us move beyond the war system, in which conflicts end with victors and vanquished, to seeking just, creative, and positive resolution of conflicts.

In order to see more clearly why women's participation in security policy formation can make these significant differences, we need to focus attention on certain feminine characteristics that have informed women's approaches to conceptualizing peace and influenced the actions they have undertaken to pursue it. Again, there are four that have particular relevance to security issues. Women's tendency to view problems of peace and security holistically, the feminist insistence on the demystification of security discourse, the feminine mode of "disarming" antagonists with respect and reconciliation, and women's proven capacity for synergizing resources to achieve more with less are all absolutely essential to the achievement of global security as defined by the feminine dimensions outlined here.

Holism, feminists insist, should be the basic framework within which we view security issues. Women's ways to peace lie in recognizing connections rather than imposing separations. The tendency to separate issues one from the other, to work on "arms control" in single, discrete steps, to concentrate on the specifics of individual weapons systems and particular conflicts that characterize current analyses of security issues seems to be an obstacle to our escaping from "the national security straitjacket" (Mische and Mische 1977). Women's insistence on viewing the issues from a global perspective, on seeing the interrelationships among the problems, confronting the general dependence on weaponry instead of adequate international machinery for dealing with conflicts, comes from their basic view of the world as a set of interconnections and interdependencies. Holism also helps to illuminate new possibilities for resolving problems viewed in this wider, more varied context.

Throughout history, women have engaged in a form of disarming antagonists, by transforming hostility, by helping those in conflict to see the conflict as a common problem, mutually damaging and threatening to all involved parties. They have helped people to understand that the origins of conflict do not reside in one party or the other, but in the relationship; that if a "win-win" nondestructive solution is to be found, the conflict must be examined objectively as a common problem and the relationship must be restructured so as to prevent such problems. It is, for example, this kind of understanding Palestinian and Israeli feminists have sought to introduce into the Middle East debate.

Disarming one's antagonist has always been seen as a way to a successful outcome for at least one party to a conflict. As women try to instruct the world about the vital need to find win-win solutions to conflicts, they also demonstrate the vital need to "disarm" all parties. Mothers have "pacified" sibling rivalry by just such processes by inducing their children to "lay down their arms," i.e., to give up the weapons with which they threaten and wound each other, most particularly their resentments, anger, and hostility. They understand that injuries must be both acknowledged and pardoned. The "kiss and make up" resolution to family quarrels mothers negotiate and the "shake hands and be friends" outcomes teachers mediate in playground fights are not far distant from the forgiveness and reconciliation in international conflicts recently advocated (Levin 1992; Monteville 1985).

Such resolutions derive primarily from an understanding that the survival and well-being of each party to the conflict depends on the survival and well-being of the other. Each is a part of a single system, a family, a school, a geopolitical or bioregion, or the human species, or the planetary ecology. The health and security of the whole depends on the conditions of its various parts. It is an understanding that leads to an appreciation that cooperation produces more benefits for all than does conflict.

"Synergy," wherein positive, constructive relationships makes the whole greater than the sum of its parts, is a mode of action long practiced by women struggling to meet expanding human needs with limited and decreasing resources. Such a feminine approach to resources is desperately needed in a world in which more and more have less and less. But these possibilities in the security area are obstructed by separation and competition, and obscured by the jargon and euphemism of the security discourse conducted by the experts and policymakers. This discourse is an insult to democracy and the self-determination of peoples that *The Nairobi Forward Looking Strategies* declared to be essential components of peace.

Demystification of this language and dispelling the secrecy of security policy that contributes to the continuation of the arms race and the exclusion of most of the public from participation in security policy making, as we shall see, has been a particular characteristic of specifically feminist peace efforts. Such change is absolutely essential if those who are affected by a policy are to even understand it, much less participate in its development. Some feminist scholars whose work will be addressed in this book have most clearly articulated this need.

All of these characteristics stem from women's ways of knowing, thinking, and decision making, also to be explored here as ways to peace. As we seek ways to achieve authentic global security, it would be well to be aware of these and to apply them to all peace movement actions and to work for their inclusion in security policy making. They help to illuminate the problems of the narrow and restricted nature of security debates and to demonstrate the possibilities for alternative ways of thinking about peace and security.

Women's Challenges to the Old Ways of Thinking

Feminine characteristics in such stark contrast to the characteristics and thinking that currently shape peace and security policies have enlivened study, discussion, and action arising from the International Women's Decade. Many peace lessons were learned as women and all seekers of peace throughout the world came to understand more fully the true meaning of Albert Einstein's well known statement that "the splitting of the atom has changed everything save our modes of thinking, and thus we drift toward unparalleled catastrophe". Women peace activists have deep concerns and anxieties about the apparent fact that the ways in which many policymakers think about peace and security issues have not changed to meet the unprecedented imperatives of the nuclear age and the realities of interdependence.

In the 1980s, a major concern of the peace movement was the tendency by some military leaders and defense strategists to "conventionalize" nuclear weapons as not qualitatively different from non-nuclear or "conventional" weapons. Dr. Stephen Kull of Stanford University, having interviewed many defense analysts, provided some examples.

> In a general way, what was particularly striking about those who described advantageous goals was the extent to which they would employ traditional, conventional concepts of war when speaking of nuclear war . . . [Kull cites a particularly Clausewitz-type response.[10]]

> A: A war is nothing but an extension of a political confrontation, and the only purpose of a war—

> Q: Of a conventional war?

> A: Any kind of war! The only purpose of the war is to remove the government that started the war, that's doing something you don't like!

> And as one defense analyst said of war in the nuclear age, . . . you would look at it the same way that military leaders have always looked at it . . . if we get into the situation, then we look at it "as a war."

> Q: What do you mean "as a war"?

> A: After the war is over somebody occupies somebody else; somebody decrees to somebody else what the government will be like. (Kull 1986, 5)[11]

Thinking in these terms about weapons that could conceivably destroy all human life, the Earth itself, seems to many women, not only peace activists, a deeply frightening absurdity. To plan defense and "security" policy so extensively on the existence of such weapons appeared to be deliberately courting a human disaster of unimaginable proportions. Women became especially vocal in decrying the apparent belief among many at the highest levels of security policy in the 1980s that a nuclear war could be won. Most of all, they decried contradictions and seeming hypocrisy in statements regarding disarmament that revealed the lack of commitment to serious consideration even of the reduction, much less the abolition, of nuclear weapons. Dr. Kull has referred to such statements as "the double image" of advocating nuclear arms control while developing nuclear war fighting capacity.

This problem was recognized by several individuals. They pointed out that it was necessary to present a kind of double image—one for each audience. One analyst referred to this as a "two-track" approach. A former high-level Pentagon official said:

'You're always dealing with contradictory audiences. At the same time you want to persuade the Soviets that there's an absolute certainty if they cross the Elbe that they are going to get caught, you want to persuade the American and the European audience that war with nuclear weapons will never be waged . . . there are inherent contradictions if you want to appear gentle and thoughtful to your own public, and tough—and just a touch irrational—to your adversary. (27)

The public too could discern such double imaging. For example, in January 1987 a *New York Times* headline declared "Defense Aide Rejects Concept of a World Free of Atomic Arms" and quoted Presidential security advisor as saying, "The foolishness of a nuclear–free world is in no way mitigated by the conditions that . . . statesmen routinely attach to its achievement in order to avoid dismissing the idea as the empty propaganda it is."

Applied simultaneously with this form of strategic thinking, however, was "New Thinking," as it was called by Mikhail Gorbachev, the Soviet premier who was the first to articulate it. The futility of dependence on nuclear weapons was publicly recognized. Indeed, in a 1988 address to the UN General Assembly, President Ronald Reagan declared that a nuclear war could not be won and should never be fought. Women's peace efforts inspired, pressed for, and supported such new thinking that ultimately led these two leaders to sign the Intermediate Nuclear Forces Treaty in 1987, considered to be a first, if very tentative, step toward nuclear disarmament. Further significant reductions were announced in 1992; but the shadow of nuclear war remained as serious proposals for an internationally controlled strategic defense initiative were put forth at a special session of the Security Council.

That the emphasis on nuclear weaponry extended to security planning in states other than the major powers became painfully evident in the aftermath of the Gulf War. The Iraqi government, technically under prohibition against pursuing such development, continued to hide evidence of its developing nuclear weapons capacity. As of this writing (early 1992), the problem of proliferation remains unchecked. The consequences of having accepted and "conventionalized" nuclear weapons continues to threaten world security.

The women's peace movement, however, has refused to accept this thinking, and the hopelessness, the resignation to the inevitability of disaster, which is the fundamental basis of such thinking. In greater and greater numbers they have penetrated the mysteries of strategic thinking and security planning. They have laid open the inconsistencies and futility that permeated so much of the thinking that underlay national security policies and negotiations for "arms accords." They noted how the objective of authentic disarmament was impeded by obfuscation and deviation from the goals that numerous statements had publicly embraced and that both the USSR and the USA had stated to the UN General Assembly were the goal of their arms negotiations—general and complete disarmament (McCloy-Zorin Accord 1961). Women activists and researchers challenged the masculine modes of strategic thinking that control the security of the world. They have pointed out some of the untenable assumptions guiding security planners, particularly nuclear weapons decision makers. The Oxford Research Group summarized what they argued to be among the most dangerous assumptions:

- all defense problems have technical solutions
- conflict is best solved by force
- threat can be assessed by counting the enemy's weapons, and not our own
- threat can be assessed by examining the enemy's *capability*, not his *intentions*
- nuclear weapons are like any other weapons
- the system is under control
- secrecy and lack of accountability are necessary and desirable
- obeying orders absolves you from responsibility
- aggression is innate
- accidents won't happen
- man-made systems are infallible (McLean 1987, p. 10)

In an article entitled "Naming the Cultural Forces That Push Us toward War" (1983), Charlene Spretnak focused on some of the fundamental cultural factors that deeply influence ways of thinking about security. She argues that patriarchy encourages militarist tendencies.

Since a major war now could easily bring on massive annihilation of almost unthinkable proportions, why are discussions in our national forums addressing the madness of the nuclear arms race limited to matters of hardware and statistics? A more comprehensive analysis is badly needed . . .

A clearly visible element in the escalating tensions among milita-rized nations is the macho posturing and the patriarchal ideal of *dominance*, not parity, which motivates defense ministers and government leaders to "strut their stuff" as we watch with increas-ing horror.

Most men in our patriarchal culture are still acting out old patterns that are radically inappropriate for the nuclear age. To prove dominance and control, to distance one's character from that of women, to survive the toughest violent initiation, to shed the sacred blood of the hero, to collaborate with death in order to hold it at bay—all of these patriarchal pressures on men have tradition-ally reached resolution in ritual fashion on the battlefield. But there is no longer any battlefield. Does anyone seriously believe that if a nuclear power were losing a crucial, large-scale conven-tional war it would refrain from using its multiple-warhead nuclear missiles[12] because of some diplomatic agreement? The military theater of a nuclear exchange today would extend, instantly or eventually, to all living things, all the air, all the soil, all the water.

If we believe that war is a "necessary evil," that patriarchal assumptions are simply "human nature," then we are locked into a lie, paralyzed. The ultimate result of unchecked terminal patriarchy will be nuclear holocaust.

The causes of recurrent warfare are not biological. Neither are they solely economic. They are also a result of patriarchal ways of thinking, which historically have generated considerable pressure for standing armies to be used. (Spretnak 1983)

These cultural tendencies have produced our current crisis of a highly militarized, violent world that in spite of the decline of the cold war and the slowing of the military race between the superpowers is still staring into the abyss of nuclear disaster, as described by a leading feminist in an address to the Community Aid Abroad State Convention, Melbourne, Australia:

These then are the outward signs of militarism across the world today: weapons-building and trading in them; spheres of influ-ence derived from their supply; intervention—both overt and covert; torture; training of military personnel, and supply of hardware to, and training of police; the positioning of military bases on foreign soil; the despoilation of the planet; 'intelligence' networks; the rise in the number of national security states;

more and more countries coming under direct military rule;[13] the militarization of diplomacy, and the interlocking and the international nature of the military order which even defines the major rifts in world politics. (Shelly 1983)

While some military states, notably in Latin America, gave way in the latter part of the decade to civilian rule, there was no significant change in the conditions outlined by Shelley. Civilian governments did not rush to demilitarize much beyond the executive. The alternatives advocated by women did not receive serious consideration.

It is true that some governments have taken some interest in nonviolent alternatives;[14] however, women's perspectives on peace and security have had little effect, due in no small degree to the secrecy that still surrounds policy making on issues of peace, security, and weapons development. The problem posed by secrecy is noted in *The Nairobi Forward Looking Strategies*.

The growing opposition of women to the danger of war, especially a nuclear war, which will lead to a nuclear holocaust, and their support for disarmament must be respected. States should be encouraged to ensure unhindered flow and access to information, including to women, with regard to various aspects of disarmament. (FLS, para. 254)

Scilla Elworthy (Mc Clean) and the members of the Oxford Research Group (ORG) in England analyzed the process of nuclear decision making and shared the results with women researchers, parliamentarians, and activists throughout the world. Underlying their work was a belief that understanding the dynamics and the secrecy of the process is a step toward women's involvement in security policy, toward democratizing the security policy making process, and ensuring an "unhindered flow and access to information." The ORG provided this overview of the weapons development dynamics and public access to information about it.

III. Why the nuclear arms race doesn't stop

- *Arms control, far from being a restraint, has frequently been a rationale for new weapons.* Cruise and Pershing II, for example, were deployed in order to be able to "negotiate from strength" over SS20s. The same rationale has been used in the case of Trident, MX and MIRV; there are indications of a similar military influence over arms control policy formulation in the Soviet Union, prior to August 1985 when Secretary Gorbachev introduced the Soviet moratorium on nuclear weapons testing.

- *Democracy, when it comes to nuclear weapons, doesn't work.* None of the five major nuclear weapons states consulted their respective parliamentary institutions before acquiring nuclear weapons. In the UK, France, the Soviet Union, and China, representative bodies still exercise negligible influence over nuclear weapons decisions . . .

- The people of these nations, in whose names nuclear weapons have been built, have had no direct say in the decisions. Only in the UK and the US have nuclear weapons been the subject of a sustained public debate, but this debate has had remarkably little practical effect on all but a few decisions.

- *Politicians aren't the real decision-makers on nuclear weapons.* Weapons now take so long to be built and are so complex that politicians are no longer in control of their development. Key decisions on the design, strategy, targetting, funding, building and deployment of the weapons are taken by much less visible groups of men. (McLean 1987, p.13)

In light of this latter aspect of the dynamic of weapons development, the ORG urges that the armament process be monitored from its earliest stages and that citizens express their concerns to the public and to the strategic researchers and planners.

Nuclear Weapons Decision-Makers

At the moment the men who make the real decisions on nuclear weapons are largely unaccountable. They carry on their work out of the public eye . . .

. . . the Oxford Research Group has identified key groups of decision-makers in each of the nuclear weapons nations. The most accessible of these groups:

Weapons Scientists and Physicists, who design new possibilities for nuclear warheads.

Intelligence Analysts, who are the sole source for assessment of the enemy threat.

Strategic Planners in Think Tanks, who devise nuclear war scenarios.

Defense Contractors, who design and make the missiles and
other "delivery systems" for nuclear weapons.

Military Strategists who have operational control and strategic
direction of nuclear weapons.

Officials in defense bureaucracies, who decide how the budget is
spent.

Foreign Policy and Arms Control Policy Formulators, who adapt
foreign policy to defense policy. (McLean 1987, p. 15)

The ORG circulated this information about groups of decision
makers to facilitate the attempts of peace groups, particularly women's
groups, to have some influence over weapons policy making. Still, the
type of information they have gathered is not widely applied, and
much of it still inaccessible.

Some researchers argue that access to relevant information is
also hindered by the mystifying language "experts" use in discussing
security policy. It is this argument that leads women to pursue the
demystification of a security issue and making possible the flow of
information called for by *The Nairobi Forward-Looking Strategies*. A
few have made extensive and serious study of the various issues and
problems involved in security policy and have begun to penetrate the
"jargon" and translate it into terms that are readily understandable
by the ordinary citizens whose lives are so profoundly affected by these
policies. Democracy is a significant value to these women, who seek
not only their own representation in the policy–making process, but
a broader representation of all whose rights to, and expectation of,
well-being related to security are determined by these policies.

Women have also been leading advocates of an integrated and
holistic perspective on disarmament as a means to security, recognized by growing numbers of citizens throughout the world as the only
effective framework, the only adequate context within which to
understand and resolve the problems. They see the central security
task as far more complex and comprehensive than reaching specific,
limited accords on arms control. The fundamental requirement to
assure global security is to do away with war entirely. The task is to
achieve the abolition of the war system and the ultimate elimination
of all forms of socially sanctioned violence.

The association of peace at global and national levels with social
justice, peace within families, safety of homes, children and

families is predominant in feminist literature. It reflects present
trends among scholars, researchers, and NGOs relating to women
and peace which put strong emphasis on alternative ways for the
promotion of peace and the resolution of conflicts through development of global sisterhood and rejection of all forms of violence,
oppression, and use of force. (JUNIC/NGO 1986, p.1)

The ultimate and fundamental value that informs women's peace
efforts is the sanctity of life, all life, including the lives of those whom
militaristic thinking designates as enemies. For example, it was
women's groups who spoke most forcefully of the callous lack of concern
for the thousands of Iraqi civilian lives exhibited in the use of excessive
force to expel the occupying forces of Iraq from Kuwait in January and
February 1991. These views and values are very different from those
that now govern security policy making. Current policy makers do not
seem to be able to envision a truly different world, one that is authentically secure, peaceful, and humane. In "The New World Order," they
seem to see a future very much the same as the present, with minor
adjustments in power arrangements still held in place by force or the
threat of force to be applied with the sanction of the United Nations. They
seldom grasp the possibilities for alternatives to arms and violence in
extreme conflict situations. Women know the world can be very
different, and they can and do envision alternative futures in which the
peoples of the world can live together so as to enhance the quality of life
for all. Women have conceptualized a peaceful world, not as one without
conflict, but as one without violence. Women's visions of the future
involve the achievement of authentic, comprehensive global security.
Such visions are evident in the emergent framework of global security
that can be discerned in women's major campaigns and actions for peace,
justice, and the environment.

The next chapters will present some of the problems and obstacles that both impede and inspire those visions. These problems
and obstacles are the background from which women project the
images of peace that are engaging ever wider groups in the struggle
for peace. A positive image of what is possible inspires many to aspire
to goals formerly believed impossible of achievement. Visions are the
inspiration of mobilization and action.

For Reflection and Discussion

Before a discussion of the issues and questions raised in this
introduction, it would be helpful to review the Universal Declaration

of Human Rights (see appendix 1), the Convention on the Elimination of All Forms of Discrimination against Women (see appendix 2), and *The Nairobi Forward Looking Strategies for the Advancement of Women* (1986). (All are available from the United Nations Department of Public Information [DPI]—see appendix 3.)

1. To start the discussion, ask for individual definitions of peace and compare them with the definition offered in this chapter. Discuss the sources of personal and popular notions of peace.
2. Are the relationships among equality, development, and peace as readily apparent as asserted in the text?
3. Ask what beliefs about women's stake in peace the students bring to this study of women and peace. What notions are added to those noted in the text?
4. In small groups, try to envision and describe a community at peace, the nation at peace, the world at peace. What conditions would be the same? What conditions would be different? What differences might women's participation make in achieving such visions?
5. How would you characterize the thinking out of which peace and security policies are now derived? How would you like to see that thinking change? How do you think the changes can be achieved? What effects did the International Decade for Women have on thinking about peace and security? Do you believe feminine modes of thinking can make a constructive contribution toward achieving global security?

For Further Reading and Study

Each chapter contains reading suggestions from which a full syllabus on women and global security issues might be constructed. The appendices include some essential UN documents, a list of relevant women's organizations, with addresses, and a bibliography on women and global security issues. These references are offered to facilitate more extensive study of the issues from diverse perspectives and to encourage the design of other courses of study.

Elise Boulding. 1977. *Women in the 20th Century World.* New York: Sage.
    The history of women's participation in war and peace activities is
    discussed, as are women's attempts to increase their political partici-
    pation. Emphasis on women's participation in nongovernmental orga-
    nizations.

Robin Morgan. 1984. *Sisterhood is global.* New York: Doubleday. Provides through voices of women themselves an overview of the global women's movements.

Hilkka Pietila and Jeanne Vickers. 1990. *Making women matter: The role of the United Nations.* Atlantic Highlands, N.J.: Zed Books. Provides an account of UN actions, conventions, and conferences intended to improve the status of women. This work is an invaluable aid to the inquiry opened here.

JUNIC/NGO (Joint United Nations Information Committee/Nongovernmental Organizations) Programme Group on Women. 1987. *Women and peace: Equality, participation, development.* Kit no. 5. Vienna: United Nations, Division for the Advancement of Women. The kit upon which this book is based would not be redundant for users of this book. The narrative here has been changed significantly, and the folios of readings contain complete copies of many of the original texts and documents this book quotes and refers to, including the UN conventions and declarations. The full series of JUNIC kits is recommended.

How to Order the Original Study Kit and Other JUNIC/NGO Kits for the Advancement of Women

JUNIC/NGO kits are available in English, French, and Spanish. Information on ordering them can be obtained from the United Nations Non-Governmental Liaison Service (NGLS), Palais des Nations CH-1211, Geneva, 10, Switzerland, or the Division for the Advancement of Women, United Nations Office at Vienna, CSDHA, P.O. Box 500, A-1400 Vienna, Austria.

Other kits available in this JUNIC/NGO series for the advancement of women: Women and Disability; Women, Health and Development; The Key to Development: Women's Economic and Social Role; Women and Shelter

Two

Negative Peace: The Continuum of Violence

Violence against women exists in various forms in everyday life in all
societies. Women are beaten, mutilated, burned and sexually abused
and raped. Such violence is a major obstacle to peace.

— FLS, para. 258

Violence: The Fundamental Problem of Peace

While a comprehensive concept of peace far more than the
absence of war is the notion that informs and motivates most of the
women's peace movement, war itself, the political uses of armed
conflict, is the starting point of the search for peace; for peace will
ultimately depend on the abolition of war, the negation of armed
conflict. The field of peace research has identified this negation as
negative peace. Negative peace, it has been asserted, is essential to
the transcendence of all other forms of violence; and, it is argued, it is
violence, not conflict, that is the core issue to be addressed in confronting the problem of war. Feminists, especially, argue that there is a
fundamental interrelationship among all forms of violence, and that
violence is a major consequence of the imbalance of a male-dominated
society. Force of various types, from the intimidation of rape to the
social imposition of dependency, maintains this balance. In itself, the
patriarchy is a form of violence.

War has always been the most well organized and destructive
form of violence in which human beings have engaged. However,
physical or direct violence, particularly military violence, in the
twentieth century appears to be more varied and is certainly more
potentially destructive than it has ever been. Armed conflict itself is
a common condition of life throughout the world. "Low-intensity
conflict," the constant and pervasive warfare that has plagued Central
America, the Philippines, and other areas where internal violent

struggles characterize politics, has become the most common form of war in our time. It is waged by governments, political factions, and "drug lords." Such "civil" conflicts, and the excessive violence that currently plagues urban society, take more civilian lives than lives of combatants, and disrupt and debase the life of entire societies. For example, gunfights have occurred between rival gangs in cities; children have been shot on playgrounds and have shot each other in their schools. In the fall of 1991, the New York Times reported that many children, some as young as nine, carry guns for "protection." While the media and policy-makers focus more on the major events of armed conflict among nations, such as that which has kept the Middle East in a constant state of hostility, these other incidents of warfare go on unabated.

Direct intentional violence of this kind is evidence of a militarized society, one in which the power of coercion is the main social currency, and one from which numerous other forms of violence are spawned. While states continue to rely on war for their ultimate "defense," they also continue to claim the sole right to use such organized violence. Maintaining the claim perpetuates the institution itself that both sanctions and inspires a level of violence that the state no longer can control.

Thus, we live in a violent society. We all are affected by it. Violence, in its linguistic form, becomes "words that wound." Bitter verbal disputes in families frequently lead to blows. Racial epithets initiate, mask, or substitute for other forms of violence. Such words often indicate the deeply felt attitudes that underlie even that violence restricted by law or social custom. Torture, the particularly vicious forms of local warfare where so often "nothing alive" is spared in an attack on an "enemy" community, the highly sophisticated and destructive weapons now used in international combat, and "the unthinkable," the desolation experienced in the wake of a nuclear attack, all originate in the language and thinking of a violent society.

Violence in its institutional or social and economic forms described as "structural violence"[1] is also profoundly characteristic of our time. Throughout the world, social and economic structures and processes from the local to the global level are serious obstacles to a decent quality of life and to the full development of the human person. Many assert that the poverty that condemns millions of the human family to lives characterized by hunger, disease, illiteracy, unemployment, and alienation is in fact a form of violence. Racism, especially when institutionalized in customary or legal structures of segregation and apartheid, is an extreme form of structural violence. The consequences of sexism produce considerable social violence, both physical and psychological. Women suffer institutionalized and physical violence, even in times of so-called peace. Some feminists believe that these forms of violence, as well as war itself, are tolerated as a means of maintaining patriarchy, inequitable privilege, and hierarchical and authoritarian systems (Brownmiller 1975; Reardon 1985; Roberts 1984; Spretnak 1983).

Cultural violence is also rampant in our times, from lack of civility on our urban streets to incitements against ethnic groups and adherents to religious or political dissidence in the news media. The popular media are replete with violent images and incidents. Films exploit warfare and physical and psychological torture, and sensationalize crime and all forms of human abuse, death, and devastation. Indeed, if we consider, as many do, the harm done to the environment to be a form of violence, then violence can be said to be in the very air we breathe.

Few members of the human family in our time are insulated from the varied and voluminous forms of violence that have characterized our century. Still, even with these conditions palpably evident, we may ask, "What is violence?" Many, particularly peace researchers and feminists, are coming to think of violence as avoidable and intentional harm. As institutional violence is a means to maintain privilege and hierarchy, so physical violence is used to demonstrate power or superiority. It is also used as a reaction to the imposition of power or superiority, as a means to maintain social or family order, to exert or restore authority, or to express anger. No matter what the form, violence represents a failure of humanity, be it in an individual or a group. It manifests limited social skills and lack of imagination and creativity, the most unique human attributes. Violence is destruction, deprivation, injury, and/or death that is deliberately executed for the achievement of a purpose and, in most cases, is not even necessary to achieving the desired goal. It is avoidable.

The notion of violence as a political or social tool has been rejected as unethical and ineffective by the advocates of nonviolent struggle and defense. Nonviolence as a philosophy and strategy is gaining more adherents among political activists, especially among women, mainly because of their particular experience of violence. Women are among the advocates and inventors of nonviolent tactics and strategies for achieving goals and purposes ranging from national defense to rape prevention.

Nonviolence has been defined and developed in struggle, in movements for national independence and civil rights, and as an approach to the resolution of long-standing, bitter conflicts such as those in Ireland and the Middle East. Nonviolence does not eschew conflict; rather, it seeks to assure that conflict, a necessary process for social and cultural change, will be as constructive as possible, conducted with as little damage as possible and without inflicting irreparable harm. Political struggle within nations is conducted nonviolently except in cases where the parties to the struggle have no strong commitment to the well-being of the entire nation. Violence is more akin to separation and factionalism than to maintaining community in the face of controversy and differences.

Democratic states are built upon the assumption that their survival depends upon the nonviolent settlement of differences within the national community. Some states have survived severe violent conflicts, but at great cost to their sense of identity and to the health of democracy; for the settlement, as in all wars, is imposed by the winning faction. The scars remain far longer than may be apparent, as was painfully demonstrated in the disintegration of the Soviet Union and the bloody strife in Yugoslavia. A just and viable world peace will depend in no small measure on the establishment and, more important, the use of nonviolent conflict resolution processes at the global level. This realization is central to women's approaches to peace.

Sex-Role Separation:
Women's Particular Experience of Violence

In a world so permeated by violence, both men and women are victims and perpetrators of violence. Both experience structural violence when their people's development is impeded by racism, apartheid, poverty, or other types of discrimination and deprivation. Both, particularly in childhood and old age, are victimized by modes of warfare that do not distinguish between combatants and civilians. The very young and the very old are less capable of fleeing from indiscriminate combat and are more likely to succumb to other hardships of war such as famine and disease. In Iraq, for example, the greatest number of victims of the devastation caused by the 1991 war were children who could not survive illness without medicine or live without adequate food or clean water. The destruction of the infrastructure of the country was a mortal blow to the children, and so it is in most wars.

Both men and women live in fear of being the prey of the violence of criminals and unjust governments. Women as well as men have been jailed in political prisons and tortured for political purposes. Male as well as female children have been the victims of child abuse and of death squads seeking to rid the business districts of cities in Brazil and Guatemala of the "infestation" of street urchins. Both men and women are active perpetrators of, or complicit, in the exercise of these and other forms of violence.

However, they also have some different experiences of violence. Men experience more the direct violence of armed combat, make up the majority of perpetrators of violent crimes, and participate more in direct interpersonal violence.[2] While some women experience violence in these ways, they also are victimized by forms of violence peculiar to women's experience. They suffer often the pain of being helpless to save their loved ones and those in their care from the violence of armed conflict and economic structures that impose cruel deprivations. They are the victims of the constant and widespread violence of sexual abuse and rape, lack of control over their own bodies, especially over their reproductive functions, of what has been referred to as the "colonization of their bodies" (Scala 1988). And they suffer, as well, from caring deeply about the plight of all who fall victim to disasters inflicted by militarism and militarization.

The militarization of the world has also institutionalized the violence of commercial prostitution and other forms of sexual slavery. However, while armed conflict has also been on the increase, it has been only one of the direct causes of higher levels of violence against women. Industrialization and corporate enterprises have also spawned new forms of exploitation and prostitution. Sex tourism and "free enterprise zones," profit-making unfettered by legal protections of labor, take a heavy toll on women.

Women, especially those who are economically responsible for families, are also subjected to intense structural violence. Although many work long, grueling hours in factories and on farms, they still are unable, because of conditions that exploit their desperation (conditions dealt with in chapter 3), to fully meet their families' and their own needs.

Some forms of sexual exploitation have been rationalized as the consequence of the biological differences between men and women, the so-called sexual needs of men. But biology can in no way rationalize the specific structural violence women suffer. The all-pervasive discrimination women have endured cannot be attributed to biological differences between women and men. Most of the violence and discrimination that women suffer is the consequence of socialization, attitudes, and values. Indeed, some feminist scholars assert that it is in the separation of human values into categories of masculine and feminine, assigned as a way of making social and cultural distinctions between women and men, that the roots and the perpetuation of war are to be found (Eisler 1987; Elshtain 1987; Reardon 1985).

In most societies, women and men perform distinct and separate social and economic functions that do not relate directly to their reproductive or physical capacities and differences. Certainly, breastfeeding requires women to be close to infants and makes infant care by women a practical custom, but there is no biological reason why all child care, nurturing of the dependent and infirm, and household chores should be done solely by women. While male musculature is usually better suited than female to felling trees and lifting heavy objects, there is no biological reason why most work outside the home or the family fields (where women have worked for centuries while caring for home and children as well), dominating the public arenas of commerce and politics, should be male preserves. Yet, for the most part, this division of labor is still widely practiced throughout the world and has defined distinct sex roles for most societies throughout recorded history. Even though some women have, in fact, played significant roles in the political, economic, and social realms, those roles for the most part have been interpreted by men and overlooked by the public. Only recently has there been any widely published scholarship focusing on women's important contributions to human history.[3] For reasons to be discussed in other parts of this book, this lack of women's perspectives and overlooking of women's experience is also seen as a cause for the centrality of war and conflict in recorded history and public affairs and, to some degree, as a contributing factor in world militarization.

Sex-role separation has also strengthened the value distinctions between men and women, a distinction that some claim predisposes women to have complied with their own subordination and prevented them from struggling against the violence perpetrated against them. Socialization predisposes men to assume and execute power and to pursue their public goals aggressively, even to the point of application of force when it is deemed necessary. Indeed, some assert that there is a masculine assumption that force is a necessary tool in maintaining social order and in the pursuit of national aims. Most societies encourage women to be dependent and submissive and men to be dominant and aggressive. This is not to say that all men and women behave in such manner, but that when they do, their behavior is considered normal, reinforced by a society that has internalized these perceptions. When these behaviors reach points of excess and exaggeration, it is very likely that aggressive, violent behaviors will erupt, and the weak will be victimized and dominated.

Social norms and laws regulate these behaviors, but the resulting values and attitudes that are produced and perpetuated are seldom checked. Indeed, they are often openly and fully manifest, as can be seen in the media and social custom. In films, textbooks, and newspapers, and on television, women are portrayed as sacrificing mothers, servile domestic workers, sweet homemakers, brainless fashion plates, unbearable shrews, evil temptresses/sex objects, and objects of violence. Even in the case of women heads of state, the media frequently find it necessary to comment on their garb or family status. The same media that glorify war, portray violence as necessary, depict combat as exhilarating and aggression as natural, particularly to men, reinforce the stereotypes that continue to cast women in the roles of dependents and victims and exclude them from full participation in public affairs. This glorification of violence and denigration of women serves to perpetuate the acceptance of both warfare and women's status as second-class citizens. The acceptance of the notion that war and violence are natural to humankind serves both to continue this glorification and as excuse for not facing the need and the possibility to abolish war. The destructiveness of the notion has been pointed out by a group of the world's leading scientists, who argue that the idea lacks adequate scientific basis. The "Seville Statement"[4] has been endorsed by UNESCO and many academic and scientific bodies.

> Misuse of scientific theories and data to justify violence and war is not new . . . For example, the theory of evolution has been used to justify not only war, but also genocide, colonialism, and suppression of the weak.

> We state our position in the form of five propositions. . . .

> IT IS SCIENTIFICALLY INCORRECT to say that we have inherited a tendency to make war from our animal ancestors. Although fighting occurs widely throughout animal species, only a few cases of destructive intra-species fighting between organized groups have ever been reported among naturally living species, and none of these involve the use of tools designed to be weapons. Normal predatory feeding upon other species cannot be equated with intra-species violence. Warfare is a peculiarly human phenomenon and does not occur in other animals.

The fact that warfare has changed so radically over time indicates that it is a product of culture . . . .

IT IS SCIENTIFICALLY INCORRECT to say that war or any other violent behaviour is genetically programmed into our human nature. While genes are involved at all levels of nervous system function, they provide a developmental potential that can be actualized only in conjunction with the ecological and social environment . . . .

IT IS SCIENTIFICALLY INCORRECT to say that in the course of human evolution there has been a selection for aggressive behaviour more than for other kinds of behavior. In all well-studied species, status within the group is achieved by the ability to co-operate and to fulfill social functions relevant to the structure of that group . . . .

IT IS SCIENTIFICALLY INCORRECT to say that humans have a 'violent brain.' While we do have the neural apparatus to act violently, it is not automatically activated by internal or external stimuli. Like higher primates and unlikeother animals, our higher neural processes filter such stimuli before they can be acted upon. How we act is shaped by how we have been conditioned and socialized. There is nothing in our neurophysiology that compels us to react violently.

IT IS SCIENTIFICALLY INCORRECT to say that war is causedby 'instinct' or any single motivation. The emergence of modern warfare has been a journey from the primacy of emotional and motivational factors, sometimes called 'instincts,' to the primacy of cognitive factors. Modern war involves institutional use of personal characteristics such as obedience, suggestibility, and idealism, social skills such as language, and rational considerations such as cost-calculation, planning, and information processing. The technology of modern war has exaggerated traits associated with violence both in the training of actual combatants and in the preparation of support for war in the general population. As a result of this exaggeration, such traits are often mistaken to be the causes rather than the consequences of the process.

We conclude that biology does not condemn humanity to war, and that humanity can be freed from the bondage of biological pessimism and empowered with confidence to undertake the transformative tasks . . . . Just as 'wars begin in the minds of men,' peace also begins in our minds. The same species who invented war is capable of inventing peace. The responsibility lies with each of us. (Adams 1991, pp. 16-30)

This widespread belief that warfare is natural and inevitable, which the Seville Statement seeks to challenge, has, as shall be noted in the sections dealing with women's peace actions, been challenged, not only by feminists but also by scientists other than psychologists, who were most numerous at the Seville Conference. The physicist Brian Easlea, for example, has indicated that the thinking underlying the development of nuclear weapons was particularly "masculine" (Easlea 1983). Anthropologists have also focused on the capacities for sociality and cooperation as equally significant, if not predominant, characteristics of human behavior. *In Societies at Peace* (Howell and Willis 1989), a volume of essays on the subject, some anthropologists attribute these notions regarding war as natural to Western culture, asserting that Western culture has become the most influential of all world cultures, particularly in the nuclear, technological age. Some also assert that it excludes the feminine more than some other cultures.

We wish to propose an alternative approach, challenging the assumption that aggression is an innate human drive. It is undeniably the case that in Western society aggression is regarded as part of human nature. But perhaps this tells us more about Western society than about human nature. We wish to suggest that we cannot assume an *a priori* aggressive drive in humans. The presence of innate sociality, on the other hand, has much evidence in its favour. Humans are *a priori* sociable beings; it is their co-operativeness that has enabled them to survive, not their aggressive impulses. (2)

As discussed in the section of this book dealing with peace education (see chapter 4), many scholars and educators have come to believe that the perpetuation of war and the behavioral differences between men and women are primarily the consequences of educational practice as well as socialization. Sex roles in general, and aggressive and violent behaviors in particular, are determined by learning, not biology. Aggressive behavior is not inevitable or inborn in men any more than peacefulness is inevitable and inborn in women. Although there is some evidence that males may be biologically prone to be more active and forceful, these traits are not necessarily destructive. A function of education is to channel human characteristics in productive directions. Both aggressivity and passivity can be directed to positive overall ends, just as, masculine and feminine attributes can be of equal social value.

Promoting consciousness of the negative aspects of sex-role separation, developing sensitivity to the emphasis of media on violence, and calling attention to the excessive focus of history on war, can make a significant contribution to peace. Working to create a more balanced view of the human experience, the human person, and to develop a more balanced and equitable socialization process could minimize violence. Both men and women are currently engaged in such efforts, but women have been among the most numerous of the voices raised against stereotyping and violence in the media, and in favor of education for peace and nonviolence. Indeed, women would have much to gain from such changes, but they work for them not only for themselves but on behalf of all people and in the realization that women, too, must change.

Women themselves, in playing out their roles as subordinates and victims, have doubtless contributed to the perpetuation of these attitudes, as they have contributed to the continuation of war by raising their sons to be good soldiers and by sacrificing lovers, husbands, brothers, and fathers to battle (Boulding 1977). Some have contributed to the glorification of violence by buying toy guns for their children, tolerating the violent types of actions portrayed in children's television, and encouraging the young in competitive games and often violent sports. Others have contributed to their own depiction as mindless sex objects, wily temptresses, and docile domestics by adopting such roles, by becoming objects for such images, and especially by accepting these definitions. For some women, encouraging their sons to join the military is a way of fulfilling a parental duty. For others, it is a route to making their own lives seem more meaningful.

Those who are concerned about both feminist issues and U.S. military buildup need to stop, look, and listen to some new friends of Uncle Sam. Among them are many tired, frustrated, and overwhelmed mothers of sons. These women encourage their sons to enlist in the service because they view the military as the only available means of shifting the awesome responsibility of their sons' welfare from themselves alone. There are two additional interwoven themes to this chapter: first, our recruiters are very much aware of such support; and second, feminists are not because they have not yet taken sufficient time to listen to mothers of sons.

As we have seen, the myth has it that "every mother entertains the idea that her child will be a hero," and the hero is, of course, a son. "A son will be a leader of men, a soldier . . . and his mother will share his immortal fame . . ." says Beauvoir. Woman as second sex, as other, as the inauthentic one, seeks to define herself in her son's deeds, and what better path than that of patriotism.

Pinky, the mother of General Douglas MacArthur, as portrayed by William Manchester in his biography of the general, epitomized this type of woman. For her, "patriotism, like piety, was an absolute virtue in its own right. The cause itself was almost irrelevant; what counted was unflinching loyalty to it." At bedtime she would tell her young son, "you must grow up to be a great man," and she would add, "like your father," or "like Robert E. Lee." That Lee and his father had fought on opposite sides didn't matter at all; what mattered was that they had fought well for the best interests of their country as they saw it. Pinky made it clear that this patriotism she was instilling in her son was also for her. (Forcey 1987, pp. 117-118)

All of this compliance contributes to a violent world in which women suffer consequences. Yet in so saying, we must be fully aware that such actions by women are not always the result of choice. As has been documented by actresses in pornographic films and some prostitutes, women are often forced into this compliance. While acknowledging women's roles in the perpetuation of their own oppression and in their contributions to the climate of violence, we must be careful not to blame the victims of this abusive system. We need to involve both men and women in the process of changing this system by integrating feminine characteristics, values, and experience into the value system of the culture, most especially into politics and the peacemaking process.

Women's perspectives, concerns, and experiences have much to offer those who seek to extract the core of violence from our society. Feminists, both men and women, have asserted that women's values and experiences have produced approaches to social relations and economic necessity urgently needed in our world today. These approaches reflect capacities that all human beings can develop, and thus they should be pursued in the socialization of all children, male and female (Brock-Utne 1989). Many believe that in women's traditionally defined roles as nurturers there are possibilities for a variety of untried ways to sustain the Earth and support her peoples (Ruddick 1989). Women's propensity for care holds the potential for us to devise ways capable of transforming our economic and social structures to adequately meet all our human needs. The feminine concern with relationship will enable us to maintain the web of interdependence, to find the grounds for common efforts among all peoples committed to the achievement of mutual security, even those engaged in conflict and competition with each other. Women's experience in creating constructive compromises can help us to move beyond a warfare mentality that insists conflicts must end with a victor and a vanquished, to a new perspective that seeks a just, creative, and positive resolution to all conflicts. It is women who may well have the most relevant social skills and capacities for achieving a culture of peace. Yet it is women who because of their sex are the main objects of the violence of our culture of war.

Domestic Violence: Crimes of the Hearth

Violence against women is universal and constant. Such violence is overt and direct, as is the case with wife-beating and rape. It is structural and institutional, as in the laws that dehumanize and deal with women as chattel and economic systems that exploit female labor. It is also subtle and surreptitious, as in verbal harassment and disguised discrimination. Violence against women is pervasive and often vicious. An Indian feminist, Madhu Bhushan (1986), gives a vivid overview of both overt and structural violence against women from "bride burning" (the murder of young wives by "accidental" kitchen fires) through stereotyping, demonstrating how it pervades the society and the culture. The following paragraphs include reference to the specific Indian problem of "dowry deaths" but could be applied to most contemporary societies.

A complex interplay of the forces of an unequal socioeconomic system and the institution of patriarchy generates an ideology and value system which seeks to propagate itself through an invidious process of socialization and structural forms of violence, i.e., institutions such as the law, media and family, which reinforce social and economic relations and roles. Personal violence against women, like rape and dowry deaths therefore only reflects the systematic violence of our society that creates conditions which are in themselves destructive. This understanding should prevent us from viewing acts of physical violence against women as isolated incidents attributable mainly to individual aberrations. Oppression of and violence against women has, very definitely, a cultural psychological, material and sociological base.

Structural societal violence, as reflected in the patriarchal family structure whose main ideological function is geared towards moulding children into sex roles, is further specifically institutionalised in the system of dowry—a concept which not merely reinforces the lower status of woman, stamping her as an economic liability, but has also of late, begun carrying within itself a possible death warrant and a sanction for psychological and physical torture of the bride at the hands of the in-laws.

In today's highly consumerist society, a bride has become a source of substantial capital for the groom and his family. When the bride fails to live up to material expectations, she is considered disposable and is either done away with or is driven to commit suicide. (p.1)

In these excerpts, Bhushan articulates a view of violence against women through the lenses of complexity and interconnectedness that bring the holistic focus to women's views of social issues. Seeing this problem and any problem of violence as "a complex interplay of forces" leads women to approach the solutions as well from the perspective of interrelationships and holism. She argues that "bride burning" is a practice intertwined within a network of attitudinal and behavioral violence perpetuated by male dominance and a belief in the inferiority of women, patriarchy, and sexism. Thus, this crime in which young Indian women were and are murdered by their spouses and/or their families, so that a second wife might bring still another dowry, was paid little heed by Indian society or Indian law. Indian feminists are overcoming that negligence.

As is made evident by the case of "dowry deaths," home and family are not necessarily refuges from direct, physical violence against women. A Canadian peace researcher reported the following statistics from North America. For every seventy women,

3 or 4 [females] sexually abused by age 18, probably by their natural, step-, foster-, or stand in-father or other male relative;

3 to 5 raped/sexually assaulted in their lifetimes, and 2 or 3 of them will be additionally injured during the assault;

2 or 3 battered by their husband; up to 7 suffering some form of physical violence at the hands of their male intimate at some point in the relationship;

In other words, between 8 and 12 of the [females] will be the victims of an assault, directed against them purely because of their gender. (Roberts 1986)

This situation is not unique to one world region. Violence in the home, particularly the abuse of women and children, is a worldwide phenomenon and appears to be on the rise. The following is reported by Lori Heise, an investigator from a major research institute:

Perhaps the most endemic form of violence against women is wife abuse. Study after study (Conners, in press) has shown that wife beating is prevalent in all societies and crosscuts all racial, cultural, and socioeconomic lines. Studies by Stojanowska and Plata and Calderon de Clavijo reported at a 1986 meeting of experts on violence in the family sponsored by the United Nations confirm that from 90 to 98 percent of spousal assault is directed at women. When women attack their husbands, it is usually in self-defense.

It is hard to make accurate cross-cultural estimates of the frequency of wife assault because it is grossly underreported, and crime statistics are seldom kept by sex. However, information from United Nations case studies (U.N., 1986) and national crime statistics indicate the magnitude of the problem.

- A 1984 study of urban victimization in seven major cities in Canada found that 90 percent of victims were women (UN, 1986).
- In Peru, 70 percent of all crimes reported to the police are of women being beaten by their partners (Seager & Olson, 1986).
- In the United States, a rape is committed every six minutes (Federal Bureau of Investigation, 1988).
- A study in the biggest slum of Bangkok found that 50 percent of married women are beaten regularly (Skrobanek, 1986).
- In 1985, 54 percent of all murders in Austria were committed in the family, with women and children constituting 90 percent of the victims (Benard & Schlaffer, 1986).
- In one study in the barrios of Quito, Ecuador, over 80 percent of women interviewed had been beaten by their partners (Kind, 1988).

- In two years (1986-1987), 18,000 cases of battering were reported to the police in Sao Paulo, Brazil (Savi, 1988).

According to the U.S. Department of Justice (Bureau of Justice Statistics, 1986), every 15 seconds a woman is beaten in the United States, and each day at least four women are killed by their batterers. In Papua New Guinea, a law reform committee ("Wife Beating," 1987) reports that 67 percent of rural women and 56 percent of urban women have been victims of wife abuse. And in Nicaragua, 44 percent of men admit to having beaten their wives or girl friends (Pallais, 1987).

Despite its prevalence, wife abuse is largely a secret crime. The legal system and the public are reluctant to get involved in what is seen as essentially a "private" matter. Moreover, societies collude in keeping marital violence invisible because its existence contradicts the idealized image of the family as a haven for love, security, and loyalty. (Heise 1989)[5]

Some theorists assert that domestic violence always intensifies in times of economic stress and unemployment, and some feminists assert that it increases in times of war.[6] Since 1960, unemployment estimated by data available from twenty-one developed countries has risen fourfold in those nations, and by data from twenty-nine developing countries has increased eightfold in those areas (Sivard 1987). Thus it is not surprising that the UN convened the aforementioned special meeting on violence in the family and that this form of violence was among the areas covered in the FLS, which called upon governments to "intensify efforts to establish or strengthen forms of assistance to victims of such violence through the provision of shelter, support, legal and other services" (FLS 288). Women's organizations such as the International Alliance for Women (IAW) lobbied for the inclusion of this issue in the FLS.

Women victims of family violence are in acute need of help. There is often no possibility for these women to ask for help from relatives or friends; and they may be too shy or ashamed to do so. They may believe that the misery and terror to which they are subjected are not only deserved, but also unique to their individual situation.

Whereas the aggressor stays in the home, battered women mostly leave in horror and despair, without money, and sometimes not even able to pay a hotel for the night. The concept of the "shelter" is part of a self-help scheme or concept, rather than a caretaker guardian one. It is first and foremost a physical refuge— a place to run to in what are often life or death situations.

In many European countries voluntary women's groups, through hard work and determination, have brought the public during the last ten years to the realization that women can no longer suffer mental and physical abuse in silence. These organizations have shown that violence in the family does exist and that, in fact, there are possibilities to help battered women . . .

Through the lobbying efforts of pressure groups, some Governments have decided to partly finance shelters for battered women. But as long as the need for these shelters and their importance is not fully recognized by public opinion, there will be no satisfactory solution for their financing. And there is no doubt that they are necessary—each one being overextended as soon as it opens.

The International Alliance of Women is of the view that women's organizations have a crucial role to play in convincing Governments of the need to support this first stage of help for battered women. Here again, as in the area of media and advertising, the weapon of community groups and women's organizations must be to raise the level of awareness. (The Consequences of Inequality, 1)

Women's groups such as IAW are now working to see that governments and community agencies at all levels provide the assistance called for by the FLS, and to help abused women to find alternatives to the physical and mental abuse that blights their lives. Resources diverted from the military might well be used to help stem this other epidemic of violence.

The issue of domestic violence points up another significant connection: The welfare of children is almost inseparable from that of women. Where women are abused in their homes, very often, so too are their children. This tragic fact was brought to the attention of the American public when it was revealed that a New York attorney, imprisoned for the death of his adopted six-year-old daughter, was found also to have regularly beaten his domestic partner, the adoptive mother of the little girl. The case was said to be typical of many similar instances of domestic violence. It is also reported that untold numbers of women remain in abusive situations in order to protect their children or because they see no other way to provide for them. Such women may perceive themselves as helpless in the face of the abuse and, indeed, often have little recourse and less information about how to find assistance.[7]

Social Violence: Prostitution

The incorporation of the developing world into the global industrial economy with its strong links to worldwide militarization has intensified still another form of violence against women, a form that can be summarized in the very brief descriptive terms of "the global factory" (Ehrenreich and Fuentes 1983) and what I would term, "the global brothel." These forms of violence have been especially inflicted on the young women of Southeast Asia, some of them hardly more than children who are sold or impressed into prostitution and/or grueling factory work. Whether resulting from impressment or from lack of economic alternatives, such conditions amount to slavery. They are dehumanizing and debilitating, causing suffering while they are endured and lasting physical and psychological effects that blight the often shortened lives of these young women and children. Commercial prostitution is a total violation of these victims, who have no more than commodity status in the military/industrial system that exploits and discards them.

It is interesting to note that if we were to record the chief locations of these global factories and brothels on a map, they would follow the same pattern of militarization illustrated in the maps in Ruth Sivard's *World Military and Social Expenditures* (1987 maps 3 and 4, pp. 24, 27). This mapping serves as evidence supporting the assertion that the more militarized a society, the more abusive it is to women. Militarization of an area, particularly the stationing of troops, leads to an intensification of such abuse, with the consequent rise of prostitution, rape, and sexually transmitted diseases. Such conditions have been specifically documented in the Philippines and other Asian countries, as cited in an article by Dr. Aikwa Ong of the University of California.

In documenting female sexual slavery, Ong (1984) provides profound insights into the nature of violence, defining it as "physical force used so as to injure or damage" or "the unjust use of power." The first is a precise definition of direct violence and the second of structural violence. It is through the unjust use of power that untold

numbers of young women and girls are kept in conditions that amount
to slavery, performing work they have not chosen, with little or no
recompense, and from which they cannot flee. Their lives and bodies
are owned, bought, and sold by "flesh traders." The following extract
from a UN report illuminates some of the conditions and processes of
this flesh trade.

> Although prostitution was and still is unknown in many so-
> called primitive societies, it is found today to varying degrees in
> all States, in all cultures and in all parts of the world, especially
> where the population is dense and where money changes hands
> frequently. Like slavery in the usual sense, prostitution has an
> economic aspect. Economic hardship is the main reason, but it
> is not enough; not all poor women become prostitutes . . . .
> Statistically, most prostitutes have been raised in broken fami-
> lies; a large number of them have been the victims of rape or
> incest. Even when prostitution seems to have been chosen freely,
> it is actually the result of coercion. That was the gist of the
> testimony given to the Congress of Nice on 8 September 1981 by
> three "collectives" of women prostitutes from two developed
> countries:
>
> > "As prostitutes, we are well aware that all prostitution is
> > forced prostitution. Whether we are forced to become
> > prostitutes by lack of money or by housing or unemploy-
> > ment problems, or to escape from a family situation of rape
> > or violence (which is often the case with very young prosti-
> > tutes) or by a procurer, we would not lead the "life" if we
> > were in a position to leave it."
>
> The rural exodus in the developing countries is a determining
> cause of prostitution. A survey published in 1978 shows that
> employment in the cities is essentially male-oriented. Thus, the
> first victims in the cities are women. In the country they have a
> role as producers; in the city their only role will be that of mothers
> and wives. Often illiterate and without professional qualifica-
> tions, they have few alternatives: to be unskilled workers in the
> few factories where the work force is largely female, to work in
> domestic service, to ply a small trade or to become prostitutes. In
> recent years this last option has been forced on many women as
> a condition of survival for themselves and their children.

Once embarked on that course they enter a state of servitude...the relationship between procurer and prostitute is one of dominator and dominated, exploiter and exploited, master and slave. The naivete of young people facilitates the task of the recruiters and pimps, who have several tricks for subjugating their victims without always using force. Among the most frequent are seduction and a fraudulent promise of marriage or of lucrative employment, followed by a demand for "temporary" prostitution to repay a fictitious debt; sometimes the lure is a contract to join an artistic tour abroad, a tour that ends in a house of prostitution; other times it is the offer of travel abroad as an *au pair* or study in a language-training centre. When force is used, it involves drugs that facilitate kidnapping and sequestration, beating, torture, blackmail involving children and threats of mutilation or murder.

Women immigrants are, as pointed out in the paper presented at Nice, the most vulnerable to exploitation. "Women who have been raped, beaten, forced to work for a pimp (as a prostitute who works for a procurer or a domestic worker in a family) or for illegal wages on the black market, are too afraid of being deported and dare not complain to the police." The supply of prostitutes has grown to meet the demand of large-scale tourism (through) sex tours, in which the services of a prostitute are included in the price the tourist pays for his ticket. Such tourism is quite plainly the worst possible image of development that the industrialized countries could project. (Fernand-Laurent 1985)

Prostitution flourishes in military areas. Brothels and street walkers are always found in locations where there are military bases or operations. Thus, the "industry" booms in wartime, as was the case in Southeast Asia during the Vietnam War. The sex tourism noted in the excerpt above is a legacy of that war; with the decline of military clientele after the war, clients were sought among business travelers and tourists. Here too is another violence perpetrated against children as well as women. Child prostitution has become a major concern of women's and religious organizations concerned with human rights violations.[8] The problem was one of the many that the framers of the Convention of the Rights of the Child sought to remedy. Prostitution is but one of the interrelated forms of direct violence, linking the fates of women and children that worsen in time of war.

The extreme sexual abuse of women in war time has been so severe that governments have suppressed the truth; and as in the case of the "comfort women", Korean and other Asian women forced to sexually serve the Japanese military, governments have refused to provide restitution to the victims. This particular case caused the Women and Peace Study Group of the International Peace Research Association to initiate a petition to declare sexual enslavement a crime against humanity.

Sexual Violence: Rape

Rape is always prevalent in time of war, not only by occupying or invading forces, but by national troops as well. Rape often compounds the tragedies borne by women caught up in armed conflict, civil disorder, and national disasters. Yet sexual violence, rape, and sexual battery, which constitute some of the most severe of all forms of direct, physical violence against women, are not limited to wartime. Most women at some time in their lives experience fear of, if not threat or actual experience of, rape. Some claim that as many as one in four women will be raped during their lives. Rape is routine in the arrest and "interrogation" of women political prisoners. Feminists claim that the threat of rape has kept women from more openly dissenting from their own oppression. Women's universal fear of rape is often unacknowledged by society. It is agreed that rape, which is found everywhere in nearly all societies, is the ultimate manifestation of the most negative aspects of sex-role stereotyping of the dominant, aggressive male and the submissive, docile female.

Feminists have also argued that society grants to men tacit permission to rape and abuse women, as a kind of preparation for military violence (Reardon 1985). There is clearly an attitude among many men that they are entitled to power over women, that women are to be at their sexual service. The revelations of the prevalence of acquaintance rape or "date rape" on university campuses and in various social situations is a particularly shocking indicator of this violent attitude. An antirape group, Take Back the Night, states that one in fifteen male university students admits to having raped or attempted rape. They illustrate the fact that committing rape is not limited to criminals and social deviants. In a poster announcing this fact, under the yearbook photograph of a "clean-cut," well-dressed young man is added "rapist" to the list of his college accomplishments such as Dean's List and Social Council. The 1991 rape trial of a nephew of a very prominent United States senator, a personable, attractive medical student, brought this fact home to a shocked public, stunned that such a person could be accused of this crime. The full extent of acquaintance rape is not known, nor are many of the hidden forms of violence and intimidation of women.

While rape is widespread, sexual harassment in various forms is even more widespread. It is an insidious form of sexual abuse that affects women in the office or factory, university or hospital, schools, the streets, virtually every area of social interaction. It keeps women constantly conscious of their potential victimization and perpetuates the sex-role stereotypes so damaging to both women and men. The Senate confirmation hearings for a Supreme Court appointee in 1991 occasioned a great awakening of the American public to the extent and severity of this misuse of male power in the workplace. The charges of sexual harassment leveled against the justice by a professor of law, a former subordinate of his, did not prevent his confirmation; but they did encourage more women to speak out and some employers to become more exigent in enforcing laws to prevent this violation of the dignity and rights of women.

Underlying all of the stereotyping and violence is the basic assumption of male superiority deeply rooted in many cultures, an assumption played out in all life circumstances, in the patriarchal family, public institutions, education, and the media. This assumption accounts for women's exclusion from full participation in the realms of power that shape politics and influence culture. Women's feelings and women's thinking about this assumption and its negative consequences must become part of the public discourse in order to overcome them. Feminists, both men and women, are challenging the stereotypes and confronting these conditions. It is women's groups, organized and ad hoc informal ones, that have initiated the dynamics of protest and legal action focusing on violence against women. A mother in India demanding justice for her murdered daughter was one of the first to succeed in bringing criminal charges for a dowry death. A women's collective in Bangalore regularly pursues evidence for bride-burning cases. Women in North America have organized massive "Take Back the Night" protests against rape. Thousands of women have marched through cities to educate and enlist the support of citizens to eliminate this and other forms of hidden violence against women.

Awareness and concern about the issue of violence against women is on the rise, as evidenced by direct remedial actions undertaken by women the world over to reverse this situation.

We are breaking the silence with manifestos and national declarations:

1985 MANILA DECLARATION OF THE RIGHTS AND WELFARE OF WOMEN

"We, women delegates coming from the various sectors of the Philippines society . . . together with all the international delegates coming from countries who came in solidarity with our struggles and convene here for the Second National Congress of GABRIELA (General Assembly Bonding Women for Reforms, Integrity, Equality, Leadership and Action) decry and condemn the double oppression and exploitation of women, manifested in the following:

- sexual harassment and actual abuse in the workplace
- institutional rape and sexual abuse of women political detainees
- institutional prostitution, sex tourism, child prostitution, unchecked influx of pedophiles and assorted perverts masquerading as tourists
- commercial exploitation of women in pornography
- individual rape
- wife beating and other forms of marital violence
- "mail-order bride system"

We have gone public . . . .

In JAMAICA, the Sistren Theatre Collective uses drama to stimulate discussion and raise awareness on the issues of violence against women. The 1977 skit, "Downpression get a Blow," focused on sexual harassment on the job. "Bellywoman Bangarang," their first major production, covered issues such as rape, prostitution, and child abuse. In "Madata" the problems of wife-beating and sexual harassment are explored.

In ARGENTINA, when a soft-drink advertisement depicted a woman with a black eye asking for a "piña" in a sexy voice (in English, she would have asked for a "punch"), DIMA (Equal Rights for the Argentine Woman) mounted its own publicity campaign with a one-page public protest in the newspaper. The campaign continues, however, since their original protest was not published in its entirety, and not one newspaper would publish their subsequent denunciation either of the omission of numerous signatures, nor of the sexist jokes and insults which followed.

We are demanding legal action . . . .

In INDIA, the Delhi Prohibition of Eve-teasing Bill deems that "when a man by words either spoken or written, or by signs and/ or by visible representation, or by gesture, does any act in a public place, or signs, recites or utters any indecent words or song or ballad in any public place to the annoyance of any woman" he is guilty of Eve-teasing.

In ZIMBABWE, The Ministry of Community Development and Women's Affairs put forward a proposal that included the following: women jurors sit on rape cases; compensation be granted to rape victims; and that sentences on rapists be speedily carried out. (*The Tribune*, Newsletter 46 of the International Women's Tribune, 1991)

Since the report quoted above was published, many more anti-rape actions have taken place in virtually all parts of the world; yet the violence continues, and most of it still remains unnoticed by the general public.

Too often this violence goes unrecognized, unreported or underreported and is therefore invisible.

- Only 1 in 10 cases of wife assault is reported in the U.S.
- Domestic violence is present in at least 70% of Mexican families but most cases go unreported according to a report by a Mexican non-governmental organization.
- In South America, it is estimated that only 1 in 20 rapes is reported. (*The Tribune*, Newsletter 46 of the International Women's Tribune, 1991)

Most feminists assert that underreporting of crimes of violence against women is in no small measure due to the lack of remedy reports are afforded by the responsible public authorities, as well as the insensitive, often cruel treatment reporting victims receive from these authorities. These frustrations and indignities are compounded by the censure of society, which all too often blames and shames the victims. Thus, much of women's action against violence is now directed at holding authority accountable and strengthening legal standards.

Efforts to strengthen international standards were initiated in 1991 by the First Women's Leadership Institute of the Center for Women's Global Leadership (see appendix 4 for address) in a call for a world campaign against gender violence and the circulation of a petition.

PETITION TO THE UNITED NATIONS WORLD
CONFERENCE ON HUMAN RIGHTS

"Violence Against Women Violates Human Rights"

The Universal Declaration of Human Rights protects everyone "without distinction of any kind such as race, colour, sex, language...or other status" (art. 2). Furthermore, "everyone has the right to **life, liberty, and security of person**" (art. 3) and "no one shall be subject too **torture or to cruel, inhuman or degrading treatment or punishment**" (art. 50). Therefore, we, the undersigned call upon the 1993 United Nations World Conference on Human Rights to comprehensively address women's human rights at every level of its proceedings. We demand that gender violence, a universal phenomenon which takes many forms across culture, race and class, be recognized as a violation of human rights requiring immediate action. (Center for Women's Global Leadership 1991)

The petition was issued and circulated in the first of an annual series of events to educate the public.

The 16 days of Activism to end Gender Violence begins November 25, International Day Against Violence Against Women and continues through Human Rights Day, December 10. It includes December 6, the anniversary of the Montreal Massacre. Please join the campaign to recognize "Violence Against Women Violates Human Rights." (Center for Women's Global Leadership, Rutgers/Douglass College)

They began the educational process by defining and giving examples of gender violence in the efforts to gain support for having it be legally recognized as a violation of human rights.

Gender violence includes rape, battery, homicide, sexual harassment and terrorism, incest, pornography, compulsory heterosexuality, forced prostitution, sex tourism, sexual torture, state violence, and the disproportionate impoverishment of women. The neglect and malnourishment of girls, female foeticide, genital mutilation, home detention, forced marriages and bride murder form particular patterns of gender violence in some countries. Where women are denied reproductive freedom, they suffer the violence of enforced pregnancy, compulsory sterilization, botched abortions and increased maternal mortality. Everywhere females are more vulnerable than males to violence, lack of health care, and economic impoverishment, all of which constitute a systematic violence to women's human rights. The murder of 19 girls and rape of 71 more in a Kenyan school is the most recent dramatic reminder of the severity and extent of such abuse in the daily lives of females.[9] (Center for Women's Global Leadership 1991)

The previously mentioned UN experts' Conference on Violence in the Family, one indicator of the international organization's concern with this issue, did make some such recommendations, asserting that domestic violence must be treated as a crime. Among detailed measures to combat the problem, the experts recommend

both short-term action to protect victims and long-term action for prevention. In the short term, victims must receive immediate assistance, the United Nations experts say. They must be assured of material aid, social services and information on their legal rights. Action must be taken to restrain offenders.

A place of refuge for victims is crucial, according to the United Nations experts. Shelters not only provide a safe place, but help make the problem visible. In countries where shelters do not exist, their function can be fulfilled by religious groups, family counseling centres and customary family groups.

The criminal justice system must play a major role, say the United Nations experts. Law, police, the courts and correctional services can safeguard women's rights and dignity. Police and court procedures must assure sensitive and humane treatment of the victim, by means including ensuring anonymity and trials closed to the public. Victims should have access to free or affordable legal aid. Doctors and police should receive special training, as they often are the first outside the family to see an abused woman. (Domestic Violence Against Women: The Hidden Crime 1989)

The Impact of Armed Conflict on Women

While there are still exceedingly few women in combat forces or armed conflict around the world, nonetheless much of the violence they suffer is a direct result of warfare. Women's actions for peace derive not only from their concern for the world, but also from their own experiences of war. Since the United Nations took up the struggle "to end the scourge of war" in 1945, there have been more than two hundred conflicts involving the use of military force. The majority of the reported conflicts took place in the developing world, which continued to be the scene of protracted armed struggles. Thus, those already most afflicted with the worst of the world's hardships are also forced to bear the major brunt of warfare in our time.

According to this same report, the majority of these conflicts are caused by internal political instability, the roots of which can be traced in some part to the demographic factors of population change rather than population increase. For example, ethnic conflicts within nations are sometimes caused by the influx of a new ethnic group that then competes with others in the country for resources and benefits. Tensions and conflicts often erupt in violence. What seems to be at the root of both the shifts and the conflicts is inadequate resources to meet human needs and the inequitable distribution of those available resources. A growing population produces an increased demand for resources to meet basic needs, and migrant populations seeking to meet basic needs for employment or food create growing social pressures and often political instability. The xenophobic violence that dampened the euphoria over the end of one-party communist control in Eastern Europe was such an instance. Interethnic violence and crimes against foreign workers and refugees were attributed to economic stress. As with other social crises and human disasters, women bear the brunt of these pressures and the resulting conflicts.

It has been asserted that many conflicts interpreted as political and/or ideological are at base struggles for basic necessities. Wars of liberation, for example, while they may be seen as partisan struggles, are invariably the consequence of people's need for bread and dignity. Women in all parts of the world have been active participants in such armed struggles, fulfilling many roles, on and off the battlefield. They have exhibited courage under fire and have been staunchly loyal defenders of their comrades-in-arms. Such women have dispelled the myth of the "weaker sex" and the stereotype of all warriors as male. Some feminists celebrate the female warrior in those women who struggle against great odds to achieve better lives for themselves and their children (Sylvester 1989). Women have fought and died for their people as well as men. Women who have participated in such struggles have experienced post traumatic stress syndrome comparable to that of men in the aftermath of warfare. However, as was the experience of women military and medical personnel in the Vietnam War, their postconflict problems were given far less attention than those of the men. Nor have women veterans received all the usual postservice benefits. Perhaps the wide publicity given to the sacrifices of women leaving families, risking combat and capture, even sacrificing their lives in the Persian Gulf War of 1991 will change these inequities. For as long as war exists, women are more and more likely to be involved in actual combat as well as support services. However, most women experience armed conflict not as combatants but as civilians caught in the crossfire. These women, too, have seen and suffered the ugly face of war, as has been noted earlier. What women most experience in armed conflict is loss—loss of property, of their means of livelihood, of family, including husbands and sons, and of their homes and even their countries. Often they are forced to take up the responsibilities of absent men while continuing to carry all their own. Many women farmers, for example, have lost their crops to both sides in a struggle. Many such women are forced to flee from their homes in fear for their lives. The violence that women suffer in normal times is exacerbated and intensified by war. Many women are among the growing percentage of civilian casualties, and, as we have established when women suffer, and children do too.

While the exact numbers may be unavailable, it is certain that the percentage of civilians killed or disabled in warfare is climbing sharply. According to studies undertaken for the International Symposium on Children and War held in Finland in 1983, among the casualties in the First World War only 5% were civilians, while in the Second World War that figure rose to 50%. This ratio now exceeds 80%. In the on-going hostilities in Lebanon, civilians are estimated to account for more than 90% of the deaths, with a significant majority of these being women and children.

It is reported that within the past decade more than 1.5 million children have died as a direct result of war. For every child killed, three more have been seriously or permanently disabled—well over four million. And it is estimated that another 10 million children have been severely psychologically traumatized by these wars and conflicts. These numbers do not include the estimated 25 to 30 million refugees and persons displaced within their countries, again predominantly women and children.

These statistics, rough as they are, clearly establish armed conflict as a leading cause of disability for women and children worldwide. Moreover, the numbers of those who are affected are not evenly distributed. Virtually all these conflicts are taking place in the poorer countries (often with arms supplied by richer nations), and the civilian victims of the violence are frequently from poor families and communities, the people who are tied to the land and cannot flee the hostilities. These civilians are more likely to be killed or disabled in the conflicts, but less likely to receive any sort of rehabilitative care if injured, particularly if they are women or children. Indeed, only three percent of all disabled children in the developing world receive any sort of rehabilitative services—and programmes are far less likely to be available in regions or communities with on-going warfare. (United Nations Decade of Disabled Persons 1983-92. *One in Ten*, Vol. 10, Issue 2-3, 1991)

Refugees are the most evident and numerous women victims of war. Indeed, the majority of refugees are women and children. Refugee women face many complex and trying obstacles to their security. In fleeing to save their lives and those of their children, they frequently encounter other dangers and trials. The plight of the boat people in Southeast Asia is one such trial. Women of all ages, usually with children, must give whatever they have to get passage on a refugee boat. The conditions on the vessels are a torture in themselves. The chances of reaching the proposed destination are often slim. But perhaps the most cruel experience of all is what occurs when the boats fall prey to pirates. If the refugees have any possessions left, they are taken, and many of the women are "victims of rape: mature women, young girls and even children who will bear the marks of this violence for the rest of their lives," writes Meryem C. Anar (1985):

Tu-Khuong Shroeder-Dao is a consulting psychologist who spent six months in Malaysia on the island of Pulau Bidong helping victims of rape: mature women, young girls and even children who will bear the marks of this violence for the rest of their lives. In a report, she explains how they will be haunted in the future by this terrible experience . . . .

. . . Added to the human drama are a whole multitude of psychological and social consequences.

A priori, rape is looked upon as an act of fate, and a certain resignation can be observed in confrontation with this "unavoidable accident"—a lesser evil in comparison with the risk of death that the boat people undergo when they are attacked by pirates. Then too, a woman will find it easier to "sacrifice herself to rape," if one may so express it, as a scapegoat in order to save other members of her family who are fleeing. She also knows that if she offers resistance, cries or struggles, she risks being thrown into the sea or being killed. In this case, her system of self-defense during a rape may consist of a loss of consciousness or memory which makes her fail to recall the event. The strongest urge, both conscious and instinctive, is to survive, even at such a high price. Nevertheless, this causes the woman to enter immediately into contradiction with the Sino-Vietnamese value system, which traditionally demands that she protect her body and her virginity. Hence, rape destroys her socio-cultural heritage, debases her, sets her apart and besmurtches the honour of her family. A significant fact is that the victim will never speak about it to her relatives back in Viet Nam. In one way or another, the woman feels herself to be cast out of society. A traveller without baggage and lacking any material possessions, she is thus deprived of her cultural identity. (Meryem C. Anar, "Boat Women: Piracy's Other Dimension, Rape and Its Consequences," *Refugees*, June 1985)

More fortunate refugees may make their way to new homes in strange lands where they will face problems of unemployment, cultural differences, language barriers, and sometimes the hostilities of local populations. Refugees often suffer profoundly from the psychological stress of the events that caused them to flee, compounded by the tribulations of their flight. The physical conditions of flight are sometimes more threatening in themselves, as was the case with the massive numbers of Kurds attempting to escape from retribution for their national uprising in the days following the formal hostilities in the Persian Gulf and the Haitians seeking asylum from political repression and murder. When these refugees are women with children and other dependents, their sufferings are multiplied by the needs of their dependents. If they are among those confined for years to refugee camps, added to all of their burdens is the hopelessness of being without freedom and the uncertainty of a future for themselves and their children. And in some cases, as in the Middle East, the camps themselves have become battlefields, so for such refugees there has been no escape. Although some refugees have ultimately made good new lives in new places, for many others their experience of armed conflicts has been an end to a life with any integrity and dignity. Yet most continue to struggle, as do the boat people. Theirs, too, is a liberation struggle, and a struggle for peace.

Reversing the Continuum of Violence: Demilitarization

Many women peace activists believe that only through a carefully orchestrated, sincerely and zealously pursued process of demilitarization can the violence of the world be reduced—all violence, the direct violence of the armed conflict arising from political and ideological struggles and the indirect structural violence of economic exploitation deriving from greed and competition. A growing number of peace researchers and feminists see disarmament and demilitarization to be as essential to the reduction of the abuse of women as laws regarding rape, family violence, and economic equity. The need to understand the links between military violence and particular forms of violence against women was highlighted by a group of feminist peace researchers.

1. We discern important connections between patriarchy, militaristic structures and values, and direct violence against individuals, especially women and children.
2. We identify a continuum of violence which links the violence against women to the violence of war.
3. We stress that the connections between the various forms of violence are an important part of the investigations that peace researchers need to make.
4. We state that rape and battering are violent atrocities peculiar to women, and the atrocities of war, repression and poverty fall harder on women than men. Women and children form a large majority of the refugees from war and repression, and form a larger proportion of the illiterate and the poor, than men. (International Peace Research Association 1983, p. 3)

The continuum of physical, direct violence is founded on war and the warmaking mentality. The continuum remains in place, feminists assert, because women and feminine modes of thought and behavior are closed out of the centers of power. This closeout, it is argued, also makes possible the extension of the continuum into the indirect forms of structural violence. Without the mitigating influence of the nonviolent and equitable approaches to public problems generally favored by women, without women's concern for social justice and equality, exploitation structures go largely unchecked, as does the tolerance of domestic violence. So long as these conditions exist, there can be no authentic security for women and, feminist peace researchers would argue, no real chance of achieving global security.

For Reflection and Discussion

1. Do you find the assertions about the interrelationships among all forms of violence convincing? Cite examples to support your response. Do you agree with the arguments relating war to violence against women? Again, cite examples.

2. Are the patriarchal family and wife abuse to be found in all parts of the world? How does family structure affect women's position? Does it provide conditions in which women might be abused, or are they protected?

3. What evidence other than the violence against women can you cite to support that there is a general culture of violence being nurtured in today's society? Is this your own experience? Is it unrealistic to presume we can do away with violence? What can we do?

4. What forms of violence against women are culture specific, and what forms are to be found in most cultures? What programs of action and forms of advocacy will be more effective globally and nationally?

5. What forms of violence against women result from war and preparations for war such as arms races and military training? Do the educational system and the military training system engender a respect for women's rights in general and human rights in times of war? How do films and media deal with attitudes toward women, particularly the women of "enemy" peoples? How do they deal with the human rights of enemies? What issues do educational and media treatment of women's rights and human rights pose for those trying to achieve peace and prevent and prohibit war? What organizations can, do, or should deal with these issues?

status is at the root of much of their suffering. Women's needs require a special emphasis if this long-standing injustice is to be overcome.

In the United States and most other countries, women have also been conditioned to want and expect less than men—in education, work opportunities, wages and even food. Men are seen as providers and therefore must have the best of what is available. Women, who usually receive little or no pay for their work as wives, mothers and family laborers, get the leftovers.

In many parts of the world women and children are more likely than men to be malnourished, because they must wait to eat until the men have finished. Where there is little protein available, the men get most of it, leaving mainly carbohydrates for the women and children. Female children fare worst of all in this regard. (Howell 1978, p. 1)

The FLS emphasized the pervasiveness of these forms of discrimination against women and the violation of virtually all of their human rights on the basis of their sex. The strategies also emphasized that the fundamental economic and social injustices borne by women were not likely to be overcome without a significant change in the patterns of world militarization. "The full and effective promotion of women's rights can best occur in conditions of international peace and security" (FLS, para. 13). In essence, then, women's rights require a profound commitment to the international order conducive to human rights called for by article 28 of the Universal Declaration of Human Rights. Indeed, all human beings have a right to peace, but women's right to peace in the light of the special violations they suffer in war makes this right an urgent necessity. Peace for women is a virtual human need.

The fundamental relationship between human rights and peace has been a cornerstone of the peacebuilding efforts of the United Nations since its earliest days: "recognition of the inherent dignity and of the equal and inalienable rights of all members of the human family is the foundation of freedom, justice and peace in the world" (Preamble of the Universal Declaration of Human Rights, United Nations, 1948). This relationship was evident in the three interrelated International Women's Decade themes of equality, development, and peace, concepts that pervade the Universal Declaration and other major landmark documents enumerating and assuring the authenticity of human rights. That relationship was again reaffirmed in *The Nairobi Forward Looking Strategies* in stating that they were built upon "the principles of equality" espoused in these documents (FLS, para. 6). However, violation of these rights are rampant, and many violations can be found among both the causes and the consequences of much of the armed struggle in the world. Militarization has almost always been accompanied by the suppression of the human rights of all and by the intensified repression of women's aspirations.

The concept of human rights as the foundation of peace is an ancient one that has influenced notions of what constitutes a good society and a healthy community as well as serving as the ethical rules for human relations. The concept of human rights today applies to all persons. *Everyone,* the term used by the Declaration, means human individuals and human groups. It calls for equity and equality to be the primary guideline for relationships among human beings in whatever form they take, from interpersonal, as between women and men, to international, as between nations, regions, and groupings of nations. These guidelines are the fundamental principles that underlie both the New International Economic Order (United Nations General Assembly 1978) formulated to redress the balance of inequality between the industrialized and the developing nations, and the Convention on the Elimination of All Forms of Discrimination against Women (United Nations 1979), designed to achieve equality between women and men. While equity emphasizes access of all groups to the economic benefits of society central to the New International Economic Order, equality stresses social and legal rights of individuals. It "is both a goal and a means whereby individuals are accorded equal treatment under the law and equal opportunities to enjoy their rights" (FLS, para. 11).

Women's economic and social rights have continued to be denied, some argue, because their legal and political rights are severely restricted, limiting their power to make policy decisions affecting economic and social matters. Consequently, women are caught in a vicious circle—they are poor because they are underrepresented, and they are underrepresented because they are poor. This situation has not changed significantly since it was vividly articulated by Virginia Woolf in *Three Guineas* in 1938.

All of women's rights have been limited because they have not been included within the general discourse on human rights. The separation, indeed, the *segregation,* of social issues and social goods on the basis of gender has been a major cause of the violation of women's rights. This separation is intensified by the distinction between private and public that feminists have emphasized in their political analysis. Two major obstacles to both equity and equality for women and the prevention of human rights abuses are the traditional notions of the "sanctity of the home" and the "inviolability of national sovereignty." Both notions impede social intervention to rectify gross injustices, and both are cloaked in the secrecy that is invoked to "protect the family honor" and "preserve national security." Both defile the integrity and honor of women and deny them authentic human security. Women have been murdered to protect the family honor or maintain the authoriity of the father, as was a case in the 1991 death of the fifteen-year-old daughter of an immigrant family in the American Midwest reported in all news media. Human rights violations by governments are subject to little interference from outside the offending nation state, the violators claiming that remedial intervention would constitute a violation of the sovereignty of their nations. As Riane Eisler points out in the extract below, a similar argument is made against the intervention of public authorities in cases of domestic violence.

Women's ways of thinking approach the issue of human rights more holistically and with more openness. Indeed, a growing number of human rights scholars and activists are calling for a comprehensive and holistic view that integrates all human rights. Such is the approach of the Decade for Human Rights Education (see appendix 4 for address), the anti-gender-violence campaign, and of feminist lawyer Riane Eisler (1990):

> The international movement for human rights has focused primarily on the rights of one half of humanity: men. Human rights theories continue to deal primarily with the so-called public or political sphere. Since women traditionally have been excluded from this sphere, this has in effect served to also exclude the rights of women from the category of rights protected from institutionalized oppression and discrimination. ... international agencies working for the advancement of human rights continue to focus primarily on the relations between men and men.

> The international human rights movement recognized that terms like "national sovereignty" or "national security" are frequently code words for maintaining a particular regime in power. But the idea that what national governments do should not be the subject of "outside interference" is both historically and conceptually a direct derivative of a far more entrenched

idea. This is the traditional tenet that the male head of the family is entitled to rule over "his" women and children without any outside interference with "family autonomy" or "family integrity," terms that are frequently also code words for the preservation of male power. Both these ideas are inherent in patriarchal or androcratic thinking, deriving from the primitive notion that "a man's home is his castle," in other words, his private autocratic domain.

Viewed from this larger perspective, splitting women's rights off from human rights may be seen to serve important systems maintenance functions in male dominant or patriarchal societies. The most obvious function is that by perpetuating the idea that the rights of women are of a different or lower order than the rights of "man," it serves to justify practices that do not accord women full and equal status. In other words, the segregation of women's rights from human rights both reflects and reinforces traditions where violations of the rights of women are not violations of either law or custom.

. . . Even more specifically, the issue is whether violations of human rights within the family such as genital mutilation, wife beating, and other forms of violence designed to maintain patriarchal control should be within the purview of human rights theory and action, particularly in social systems where women have traditionally been confined to the private or familial sphere.

Reduced to its simplest and most basic terms, the underlying problem for human rights theory, as for most other fields of theory, is that the yardstick that has been developed for defining and measuring human rights has been based on the male as the norm. The fact, of course, is that women are half (globally actually the majority) of the human population. The life experiences that are for either biological or traditional reasons typical for women are both similar to and different from those of males. The development of what may accurately be described as a theory of human rights therefore requires both a female and male yardstick for the protection of human rights.

. . . As the First United Nations Decade for Women evidences, women all over the world are today asserting that the same human rights standards that are already widely applied to the relations between men and men should apply to the relations between women and men. One result has been the UN Convention on the Elimination of All Forms of Discrimination Against Women, adopted shortly before the midpoint of the Decade. Because it expressly addressed violations of the human rights of women, the Convention is a potentially pivotal turning point in the human rights movement.

The Convention on the Elimination of All Forms of Discrimination Against Women was the first UN document to recognize expressly that, despite other international conventions against discrimination, violations of the human rights of half of humanity still remain generally ignored. It was also the first UN instrument to deal comprehensively with all aspects of women's human rights,[1] to establish standards that are binding on states parties (i.e., ratifying nations), and to set up the machinery for exerting pressure on national governments to abide by these standards. In specific, although still largely unnoted, respects, the Convention addressed some of the major theoretical barriers to a unified, and operationally effective, theory of human rights.

. . . The recognition that women's rights are the leading edge of human rights is both operationally and logically the prerequisite for the kinds of actions required to lay the foundations for a just social order. A unified theory of human rights encompassing both halves of humanity is essential if a basic respect for human rights is to become firmly rooted. Only then can the unfinished struggle for equal justice for *all*—the struggle for human rights—be completed. (191-203)

Double Discrimination: Sexism and Racism, the Case of Apartheid

As Eisler demonstrated, the legal rights of women throughout the world are still severely restricted, the Convention on the Elimination of All Forms of Discrimination against Women notwithstanding. In their 1990 annual report, the UN Commission on the Status of Women noted the alarming level of violence against women and the excessive burden borne by women in the growing world economic crisis. They attributed both circumstances to women's continued "second class citizenship." The Forward Looking Strategies offer some analysis for the causes of these legal restrictions and other limitations on women's rights. They cite, among other causes, poverty and underdevelopment resulting from imperialism, colonialism, neocolonialism, racism, and apartheid (FLS, para. 44).

The perpetuation of these conditions can also in some part be attributed to the fact that "women by virtue of their gender, experience discrimination in terms of denial of equal access to the power structure . . . differences such as race, colour and ethnicity may have even more serious implications in some countries, since such factors can be used as justification for compound discrimination" (FLS, para. 46). Often referred to as the "double burden of discrimination" is the exclusion of many women from the benefits of society on the basis of both sex and race or ethnicity. The double burden is suffered by some women in most ethnically and/or racially mixed countries.

There are few ethnically diverse areas in the world where race and ethnicity have not been the basis of discrimination. Ethnic diversity in most countries can be traced to one group's gaining control of territory inhabited by another group, as in cases of imperial expansion, or to immigration, voluntary and involuntary, of people who enter a territory at a disadvantage, being without means or not being familiar with the language and culture of the land to which they have immigrated. The disadvantaged are more often than not exploited by those who have more power. The exploitation is rationalized by arguments asserting the inferiority of the exploited. The rationalization of exploitation on the basis of race is the essential premise of racism. Women's subjugation, argued on the basis of their alleged inferiority to men, is the premise of sexism. Women of exploited colonial or "minority" peoples are thus victimized by both racism and sexism.

A third form of discrimination, colonialism, forces millions of women in developing countries to carry a triple burden. The quintessence of all multiple burdens of exploitation carried by women, however, is apartheid, a system that has repressed all human rights, through policies of abuse inflicted by the militarism of a police state, which the world community has tolerated for generations in the name of "national sovereignty." The abuses of women's rights under apartheid have been excessive.

> Women and children under *apartheid* and other racist minority regimes suffer from direct inhumane practices such as massacres and detention, mass population removal, separation from families and immobilization in reservations. They are subjected to the detrimental implications of the labour migrant system pass laws and of relegation to the homelands, where they suffer disproportionally from poverty, poor health and illiteracy. (FLS, para. 259)

This description of apartheid's effects on women summarizes in one situation most of the trials women must bear in an unequal and violent world. This system is the very antithesis of economic and social justice. Apartheid is absolute peacelessness. The crime of apartheid is an especially instructive instance of a major premise of the Universal Declaration of Human Rights that relates justice to peace, that "if man is not to be compelled to have recourse as a last resort, to rebellion against tyranny and oppression, then human rights should be protected by the rule of law" (Preamble, Universal Declaration of Human Rights).

The practices, conditions, and social and economic consequences of apartheid are the most extreme forms of racism. They are tantamount to slavery, the major difference being that the Europeans who enslaved the inhabitants they found in southern Africa did not export them as labor to overseas colonies. They imposed and maintained the enslavement within the colony they took as their own state. South Africa came into being through a colonial war, not a revolution or an independence movement. The war was settled in favor of the British over the Dutch with whom they struggled for control of lands both claimed as territories, but the British traditions of rights evolved since the thirteenth century were not extended to the native blacks. The racial separation and oppression espoused by the Dutch Boers became a primary principle of the political party they founded, to pursue their interests within the Union. The accession of this Nationalist party to power resulted in enacting the system of segregation into the laws of apartheid. Ironically, these laws were passed in the same year that the UN General Assembly adopted the Universal Declaration of Human Rights, 1948.

The bitter fruits of racism were also cultivated in the seventeenth- through nineteenth- century slavery systems of the Americas. African women, men, and children died by the thousands as they journeyed as human cargo across the Atlantic. The experience of slavery was horrendous for all the enslaved, but in this case, too, women endured additional hardships. Recent scholarship is uncovering the special and distinct abuses suffered by slave women in the American colonies and into the era of slavery under the independent American nations. Sexual abuse, not only occasional rape, but the continued and systematic sexual exploitation of slaves by masters and overseers, resulted in a population that bore the evidence of European as well as African ancestry. While the lighter skin of mixed heritage provided some advantage in the racist culture of the Americas, it gave no relief from the fundamental conditions of racism and slavery. So, too, under apartheid, a strict system of racial classification and segregation, those classified as "colored" because of mixed heritage have not been so abused as the "blacks" who appear to be of exclusively African heritage. However, it is the white population that is in control and holds all the privileges and advantages.

Thus, the black women of South Africa, who into our own time endure abuses tragically similar to those borne by slave women, suffer the general disadvantages of belonging to the most oppressed racial group in addition to the special oppressions inflicted on women. They have been separated from their own families as they cared for the children of white families. They have been sexually exploited, as evidenced by the generations of "coloreds" born notwithstanding the laws of apartheid prohibiting sexual relations between the races.

In spite of the systemic changes occurring in South Africa and the official dismantling of segregation, black women continue to suffer the poverty and exploitation of apartheid. Their entrance into the cities previously restricted by the pass laws that made illegal their efforts to join husbands from whom so many endured long separations, is still limited by poor and inadequate housing. Black men's low-paid labor was wanted in the townships, but neither women nor men had benefits or assurance of tolerable working conditions. Black women still work without adequate protection of their rights as domestics and in the informal sector. They have no child-care facilities, nor safe contraceptive methods, and are subject to sexual harassment, conditions not unknown to millions of poor women everywhere. Some black women are forced into prostitution.

Under apartheid, these conditions were imposed by law, a law against which black women have valiantly struggled in the townships and the homelands, where they organized women's groups such as the Magwali and Magopa to improve their circumstances. Excerpts from a short account of black women's resistance to apartheid, a struggle that continues, appears below.

I might recall that the African women were the first to carry on organized resistance on a large scale against the obnoxious pass laws way back in 1913, and that was the first glorious episode in the modern national movement in South Africa. In the 1920s and 1930s, for various reasons, the African women were the most militant leaders in the trade union movement which organized a million workers in struggle.

On 9 August 1956, the women organized a national, multi-racial demonstration in Pretoria against pass laws—a historic demonstration which required tremendous organizational capacity.

That was one of the greatest demonstrations under very difficult conditions in South African history. I remember also a demonstration of Indian women on UN Human Rights Day. Police sent their dogs to attack and pull their saris, but they stood firm.

. . . there was the great demonstration of African schoolchildren in Soweto on 16 June 1976. The children decided to defy the police batons and guns, and many hundreds were killed and wounded. I can think of nothing like that massacre of children in history. But what did their mothers do? Did they stop and scold their children for getting into trouble with the police? No, they stood by their children, in spite of all the pain and anguish, and brought out the adults in support. All of us, all over the world, should bow our heads before them.

You have heard of young freedom fighters Solomon Mahlangu and three others who were executed in South Africa. They are heroes, but equally heroic are their mothers who stood by them. They did not tell their children to confess or beg for mercy and save their lives. They declared that they are proud of their children and will carry on the struggle until they meet their children in heaven. They too deserve our humble tribute. (Reddy 1984)

Some women under apartheid actually joined the armed struggle, and many used all possible nonviolent means open to them. In the townships, they were killed or injured. In the cities and elsewhere, they have been jailed for their efforts at labor organizing. Even though only about a quarter of black women in South Africa live in urban areas, their efforts at labor organizing were an inestimable factor in bringing about the political and social changes that have made possible the 1990's initiatives to overcome apartheid.

Human Needs as Human Rights

Women's approaches to human rights have been deeply influenced by the notion of needs fulfillment as human rights that are essential to security. Feminist human rights advocates recognize that justice and effective development require women's full participation in society and politics. The relationship between peace and economic and social justice are issues that affect all of humanity, not just women, but without the contributions of women the significance of that relationship is not likely to be realized. The circumstances of women, their responsibilities for meeting human needs, and their impact on the welfare of the entire world society has become a most significant and instructive factor in development planning. For example, the failure of the UN Development Decades to meet their articulated goals has been attributed in part by various respected development planners and economists to the omission of women's participation and the lack of a human-needs perspective in goal setting and strategy planning. After all of the efforts of over two decades of international cooperation for development, the women who met in Nairobi warned that, "if current trends continue, the prospects for the developing world . . . will be sombre" (FLS, para. 24).

The present and potential wealth of the world with its technical capacities provides the vehicle for changing this situation. The realization of most human rights is fully possible in our own time. Why then do we still live in a world in which so few children are currently born into the expectation that their basic needs will be met? Among those few, why are the expectations of girl children considerably lower than those of boys? For example, a UNESCO study shows that 25 percent of girl children do not survive to the age of fifteen, largely as a result of neglect and nutritional deprivation resulting from the preference for male children. Girls will grow up to be the majority of the Earth's poor, yet they will be the minority in the policy-making councils in whose power it is to commit the world's wealth and technology to meeting human needs, to the full pursuit of an economically and socially just, nonviolent world. Efforts at development have clearly demonstrated that women's economic and social rights are impeded in no small measure because their political rights are denied.

> Hunger and poverty can be eliminated only by facing the conditions that cause and perpetuate them. Discrimination against women is a major cause of their hunger and poverty—and the hunger and poverty of children. Women, wherever they live, have little control over their political and economic lives. Full and equal opportunity for women to participate in and benefit from development will depend on fundamental changes at all levels in all countries. These include changing the attitudes of men and women about male superiority. And to gain the respect that true equality implies, women need, among other things, a fair measure of political power. (Howell 1978, p.3)

A number of women social and political activists are inspired in their struggle against the somber prospects of current trends by a vision of a world in which this situation has been drastically changed, a world in which conditions of equality in political participation, economic and social justice, and nonviolence are the norm. Many of the aspects of a peaceful society underlie the formation of our concepts of human rights.

As the articulation of the various generations of human rights laws has derived from recognizing the denial of certain human needs, political, social, and economic, so women's visions of an economically and socially just, nonviolent world arise from the lives of deprivation now endured by millions of the world's women and their dependent children. These conditions of deprivation represent a major constraint on the achievement of peace and security, and an obstacle to the full realization of economic, social, and cultural rights, condemning many to poverty, illiteracy, unemployment, and ill health. All of these conditions become even more severe when war and violence prevail, making the obstacles to meeting basic human needs even greater and compounding the human suffering of poverty with death and destruction. Even in the absence of actual armed conflict, preparation for war and the expenditure of vast resources on armaments, as will be illustrated later in this chapter, inflict mortal wounds on society's ability to care for the vulnerable and to meet fundamental human needs. These factors of the escalating cycles of arms expenditures and worsening poverty and unemployment have inhibited the possibilities for peace, and the participation of women in peace and development, and have been a major constraint on all developmental processes. As development come to be considered a human right,[2] such conditions represent gross violations of human rights.

Because the vast majority of the world's poor and oppressed are women, all of the Earth's most vulnerable who are dependent on the care and work of women are likely to be poor. To deny women's rights is in fact to deny the rights of the majority. To relieve the misery of the world's children, aged, ill, and handicapped, the condition of women must be radically changed. The advocates of the rights of children and the International Convention on the Rights of the Child clearly articulate this dependency.

With all that has been achieved in research, standard setting, and the success of many small women's development projects, the life expectations of female children, not only in India (featured in the UNESCO study) but worldwide, have not significantly changed. "Girls are born with less of a chance for full development than boys" (Howell 1978, p. 2). There may now be fewer women farmers, more having lost their land to multinationals and agribusiness; more low-paid, short-term female industrial labor and even more female-headed households or families, especially in war-torn areas. Although there are more women in politics and the professions, the general picture has not changed for most of the world's women. Many still lack the basic necessities of fundamental human security and the most basic of rights, the right to food.

Food and Ecological Security: Fundamental Needs and Basic Rights

Protection of human rights is essential to authentic human security, so as to assure the expectation of respect for human dignity and fulfillment of human needs. The international community validated human dignity in the Universal Declaration of Human Rights and, through the development of "food security" programs and policies, it recognized the significance of meeting basic human needs as fundamental to the achievement of global security and peace. The significance of the concept of food security and its inextricable relationship to women and peace and to human rights as economic and social justice has been tragically illustrated by the African famines and food crisies. As the 1945 bombing of Hiroshima has served as a vivid and painful image of the need to achieve authentic "nuclear security" through the prevention of nuclear war and the ultimate elimination of nuclear weapons, the African crisis has been an anguishing lesson in the need to prevent famine and eliminate hunger by achieving food self-sufficiency among the world's peoples. Concern with this dimension of security has led to intensive study and research.

The deeper analysis of the food security problem, as well as grass-roots approaches to agrarian reform and rural development, has made it clear that simply increasing production and creating and distributing emergency food supplies is not enough. A new broader concept of World Food Security was outlined by the Director General of FAO in 1983. The specific aims of any broader approach should be three-fold:

- to ensure production of adequate food supplies;
- to maximize stability in the flow of supplies; and
- to secure access to available supplies for those who need them.

... At the present time of severe drought across southern Africa, South Africa's policy of destabilization has threatened legitimate neighbouring governments and disrupted food production and distribution networks. In the contemporary political economy of Africa, food is being used as a weapon of international power politics. (*INSTRAW News,* n.d., 19)

A decade after this statement by FAO conditions in Somalia and the Sudan show war to be linked to famine, as cause, consequence, and strategy. Clearly, the issue of food security has become a strategic concern that is profoundly influenced by political and military factors. Nations use food as a weapon in political conflicts. Some have even suggested that in a future in which war still exists it may become not only a weapon, but the objective of wars as it was in centuries past. Nations may resort to war to feed their peoples. Yet in so doing they inevitably reduce the total world food supply. This too has been made evident by the African crisis, in that the crop disasters caused by drought have been exacerbated by armed conflict. Food supplies are seized, and, often destroyed, land is laid waste, and farmers are displaced. New classes of refugees are created, most of them women, fleeing death by starvation and/or by battle. The African crisis has shown that, far from enhancing human rights and increasing security, war and the threat of war reduces them. Security at its most fundamental level, that is, the sustaining of the life of a community, cannot be maintained under conditions of war.

It is equally clear that these threats to security are in almost every way "man-made," for women as a result of the denial of their political rights have virtually no say in strategic planning and military policy making. Nor have women significantly influenced the economic policy making that drastically altered the ecological balance of Africa, leading to the "natural disaster" of drought. From the days when Roman soldiers made way for the deforestation of Northern Africa, until a European military enforced a colonial rule that ultimately made way for dismantling the traditional, self-sufficient, female-run agricultural systems of Africa, the underlying policies have been conceived and executed without the participation of women. Authentic global food security depends on peace, international cooperation, and women. Women are responsible for 40 to 80 percent of all agricultural production in developing countries. Africa represents the higher range in this scale (*INSTRAW News,* n.d., 22). In Africa, the links between food security and ecological security are most evident.

As more and more men move to the cities, Africa's rural women bear increasing responsibility for the environment.

Even at a young age, the Burundian woman's worth is judged in terms of how she exploits nature. The more products she is able to extract from the land for the survival of her family, the greater her "value." The criteria for her "marriageability" include her tenacity in the fields, and her commitment to collecting fire-wood and discovering arable land. In neighbouring Rwanda, the dowry offered for a young girl is higher in the north, where women's participation in production is considered an *"added value."*

These two examples can be found all over sub-Saharan Africa with a few nuances here and there. They highlight the central role played by rural women in an economic system based largely on agriculture.

Indeed, the growing responsibility of these women for protection of the environment, was the theme of a five-day long seminar held under UNESCO's auspices in Bujumbura (Burundi) from April 8 to 12, 1991. (The Future is in Their Hands 1991)

The director-general of the United Nations Food and Agriculture Organization (FAO) has provided an excellent concise definition of food security as a situation in which "all peoples at all times are able to buy or grow the basic food they need." As hunger prevails in the villages of the developing world, in the refugee camps of Africa, the Middle East, and Central America, and stalks the streets with the homeless of the world's cities in even the "wealthiest" nations, the world is far from a condition of food security. Nor will we attain it so long as wars rage and resources are consumed in arms production and war preparations, and so long as women's rights are not respected and women's needs are not fully represented in food production and distribution planning. Women's participation in a peaceful climate is as essential to food security as food security is to authentic global security and world peace. Women activists argue that food security can be achieved. While women may always have known this intuitively, the research and new knowledge produced by the UN Decade for Women have provided the evidence that it is actually possible, given the political will and allocation of resources needed. Thus women cherish an image of a world in which children, girls as well as boys, are adequately fed, and in which the basic human right to food is recognized as a major policy priority.

Issues of food and famine arise from issues of the environment and mistreatment of the Earth's agricultural lands. The security expectation that our planet can sustain life is in dire jeopardy. In the nearly forty years since the contemporary American environmental movement was alerted by Rachel Carson's *Silent Spring* (1962) to the poisonous and destructive uses of pesticides, the United States and other nations have continued to abuse their arable lands so that the Earth's topsoil is so badly depleted it must be restored if it is to feed the world's peoples. Food security depends on ecological security, and ecological security depends on global cooperation. The environmental crises have demonstrated the limits of national security in the face of impending ecological disaster (Mische 1989). Neither food security nor ecological security can be achieved so long as governments seek to fulfill protection expectations by excessive military measures and degrade the environment through weapons testing. It was for this reason that the 1991 Women's Congress for a Healthy Planet put such great emphasis on demilitarization.

More than 1,200 women from 83 countries gathered to examine the most important environmental and developmental issues facing women and the world in the 21st century in order to ensure their concerns be addressed *directly* at the upcoming United Nations Conference on Environment and Development in Brazil in June, 1992. A "Women's Action Agenda" for the 1990s drawn up at the Congress has been disseminated . . . .

[It] delivers a bold and stinging indictment of the priority given to military might by most nations, citing militarism's tremendous human and environmental costs, and offers solutions that deserve close attention at the Earth Summit.

The Agenda calls for:
1. An immediate 90% reduction in military spending.
2. An immediate halt to nuclear testing.
3. The creation of a Global Nuclear Test Ban Treaty.
4. An end to new nuclear research, development and production.
5. An end to uranium mining.
6. The phasing out of nuclear power in favor of energy efficiency, solar, wind, and water power.
7. The prompt cessation of all radioactive nuclear waste exports to developing countries and poor communities.
8. The dismantling of existing nuclear weapons.
9. Greatly increased regulation of the international arms trade.
10. A ban on food irradiation.

. . . When a critical mass of women finally become equal players in determining public policy, progress toward a world beyond war will become possible. The environment will be treated with the respect it deserves, and the problems of the vast inequality in distribution of land and wealth will be dealt with more fairly than they are now. (Plotnick 1991, p. 6)

Health, Education and Employment: The Conditions for the Enjoyment of Rights

Women are ready to struggle for peace and the security goals of an authentically secure world where all human rights are respected, but their effectiveness will depend on having their own rights recognized and their own needs more adequately met, especially their needs in health, education, and employment. These conditions are rights in themselves and also the requisites for the pursuit of other human rights. As women's rights and needs in these areas are denied, so too are the rights and needs of others whose care is entrusted to women.

Women, who are the major health care providers of the world, must have adequate health care themselves if they are to have the physical capacity to meet the needs and defend the rights of others. As comparatively few of the world's people have access to professional medical care, women provide most health care. Even in areas where such care is available, women provide the daily health needs in the family. Yet women's own special health needs are, in general, inadequately met. This situation prevails in both industrial and developing countries and is especially acute among the poor. On the average, women more than men tend to be malnourished, and consequently many women in the developing nations suffer from nutritional anemia (Sivard 1983). This condition in itself makes childbearing more taxing and difficult. Repeated, closely spaced pregnancies, and pregnancies among very young women barely out of childhood themselves, also impose a great stress on the health and well-being of women, especially in the developing nations (Sivard 1983).

The failure to meet women's health needs is a violation of their human rights and consequently of the rights of others. The health and well-being of others depends on that of women, on their being able to do their work in the fields and factories, to maintain homes and families. In the case of infectious diseases, women's health is vital, and their rights are also crucial.

A recent Expert Group Meeting on Women and AIDS, organized by the Division for the Advancement of Women in Vienna from 24 to 28 September 1990 and co-sponsored by WHO and the

Government of Sweden, concluded that women without basic
human rights were indeed particularly vulnerable victims. . . .

According to the documentation, the "lower status of women within
the family and society, the lack of independent income and the
social and economic dependency on men" heightened women's
vulnerability to HIV infection since they were less able to control
the "personal and socio-economic circumstances which put them at
risk, creating a feeling of powerlessness, both in personal relationships and society."

AIDS education campaigns were repeatedly criticized by these
experts for proceeding on the naive and false assumption that
women could exercise more influence over sexual practices than
was actually the case. In reality, they maintained that women at
the bottom of the socio-economic ladder often did not enjoy even the
most basic human rights.

Even in so-called "developed" countries, women were objects of
discrimination in this life-threatening realm: their rights to safer
sex went socially unrecognized and thus unenforced. Even the
mere suggestion that their partners use a condom often led to
personal rejection or even violence. This situation, the experts
concluded, must be remedied before any real progress would be
possible. ("Women and AIDS" 1991)

The concept of well-being as the essence of security makes health
a useful notion in judging all components of comprehensive, authentic
security. Rosalie Bertell, a health profesional well known for her work
on the hazard of low-level radiation, put forward a proposal based on this
notion that has been taken up by the women's environmental movement,
and is discribed by a Norwegian peace advocate, Eva Nordland.

Rosalie Bertell has observed that "the primary concern of men in
our society is the economy . . . they have defined their role in the
world as taking care of money and economy . . . , leaving to the
women . . . air, land, food, water, babies, homes and everything
else . . . . A point has been reached where this kind of crippled
establishment that is focusing on money . . . cannot continue, so it
is crumbling, crumbling slowly." (Nordland 1991)

So, as reported in Nordland's paper, Bertell has proposed that
women present alternative economic assessments accounting for the
health of the environment. These assessments she calls "report cards."

The report cards as means of evaluation concern 1) a healthy natural environment and 2) a healthy man-made[3] environment:

- The first area to be evaluated for the individual country, is that of a healthy natural environment—the quality of water, air, soil, forests, animal life.
- The man-made environment is described through the report cards in four systems: the value system, the political system, the national household system (how the resources are used), the human development system. Evaluation of these four types of systems takes into consideration a broad range of issues important for human beings in all parts of our global society.
- To evaluate the health of these systems a scale from 0-4 is to be worked out. In addition, certain quantitative data are to be written up (as far as it is possible to get the information from individual countries).

The scale is organized as follows:

(4) "The system is on the whole healthy, and efforts are being made to improve it."
(3) "The system is still in good condition, but threatened in different ways."
(2) "The system has serious problems, but efforts are being made to improve it."
(1) "The system is deterioarting, but plans are being made for improvement."
(0) "The system is not working and no attempts are being made to improve it."

These five marks are used for the natural environment and the four areas of man-made environment. It is important to remember that the marks are given as an evaluation and are bound to be approximate. (Nordland, p. 4)

   Bertell's assessment scheme reflects the feminine characteristics of holism with its comprehensive approach to economic well-being and the anticipatory and futuristic perspective women bring to the consideration of all issues of global security.

   In addition to health, women's education and employment needs are vital to global security and fundamental to the achievement of the goals of the Women's Decade, forming the center of study and activity during the latter half of the decade. The reasons for the concern are

made evident by many statistical studies of the education gap between
males and females, indicating in the mid-1980s a literacy gap of 28
percent and an educational enrollment gap of 33 percent in the third
world (*INSTRAW News,* n.d., n.p.). Thus, nearly a quarter of the
female population is illiterate, and over a third are never enrolled in
school. Women, the first educators of the young, cannot help mold
young minds for acquiring the sophisticated knowledge necessary to
function constructively in the twentieth and twentieth-first centuries
if they themselves are ignorant and illiterate. The right to education
of most children is dependent on women's right to education. As the
proverb (attributed frequently to Africa) says, "Educate a woman and
you educate a family." And, it might be said, you assure higher
standards of health to that family.

> Salaan, though frightened at seeing her child in such a state,
> mixed a spoon of salt and four spoons of sugar in two bottles of
> boiled water and made her son drink it.

> After two or three days, the diarrhea was gone and Naroi's smile
> was back.

> Delivering such a simple form of first aid to remote villages such
> as Amper Phnom, 60 kilometers west of the Cambodian capital
> Phnom Penh, remains a difficult challenge even for sophisti-
> cated international aid agencies.

> While the cure costs no more than 6 cents, one of the main
> obstacles is to get the message through to the mothers. The
> number of illiterate women around the world is high; while about
> one-fifth of men cannot read or write, one-third of women are
> illiterate.

> These women cannot read medicine prescriptions, or simple health
> instructions on the importance of breastfeeding, vaccinations and
> how to prepare clean food for young children. They want the best
> for their children but they cannot obtain the necessary information
> on how to help them be healthy. Salaan learned about the simple
> sugar, salt and water cure, also called "Oral Rehydration Therapy
> (ORT)," in a literacy class. Held in the shade under a tree, the
> classes gave instruction in not only how to read and write, but also
> in how to better take care of her child.

> Salaan's new-won knowledge saved her baby's life, but if her son
> had had the same illness a year and a half ago, she might not

have succeeded in giving him the right treatment. Then, Salaan did not know that diarrhea can lead to dehydration and even death. She had never been to school, could not read or write and had no knowledge of sickness. She was brought up to believe that sickness is caused by evil spirits.

"I don't have parents to teach me how to raise kids," says Salaan, "I don't have medicine either. The only thing I can turn to is what is written in the textbooks."

Salaan's story illustrates the clear link between a mother's education and the health of her children. UNICEF reports that on average, every additional year a mother spends at school is associated with a fall in the infant mortality rate of approximately 9 per 1,000. Two-thirds of the fall can be directly attributed to education itself.

Over 24 separate studies in 15 different nations yield similar results. (Literacy Means Survival 1990)

Lack of education contributes to unemployment and low pay. Women who are the sole support of so many of the world's families cannot provide for those dependent upon them without an income assured by adequately recompensed labor undertaken on their own or under the employment of others. The facts and figures on employment are equally strong evidence of discrimination against women (ILO 1986). The female share in the total "economically active population" is not expected to rise significantly by the end of the century, remaining steady in the "less developed regions" and rising only about 5 percent in the "more developed regions." Women, for the most part, tend to be employed in lower-paying jobs, a situation perpetuated by "recruitment procedures, and training and promotion policies which favor men" (Sivard 1983). Equal employment rights, a major necessity for overcoming discrimination against women, is a concern of the International Labor Organization (ILO), which has made considerable contributions in the field of economic and social rights.

Job segregation and the corresponding wage differentials between men and women are found in all countries, irrespective of their level of development and socio-economic organisation.

There are many factors that account for this situation. First, women are often treated unequally, when they apply for a job—

particularly after a period of absence from the labour force—as well as in their placement, in dismissal and in promotion. Secondly, women are concentrated in sectors and occupations where pay is relatively low. This is the case in industries such as textiles, clothing, leather and food and in services such as education, health, retail trade and tourism . . . .

Even if girls spend the same number of years in school as boys, they tend to be concentrated in non-technical fields regarded as "female" spheres of activity. In addition, men often have better access to training than women. Yet another cause is the domestic duties of women. Even if women have a full-time job, they are still considered mainly responsible for housekeeping and feeding the family, and for bringing up the children and supervising their education. The time and energy spent by women on these domestic tasks can adversely affect their performance on the job, induce absenteeism, discourage them from raising their qualifications and make it difficult for them to pursue a career . . . .

Since young women have inadequate and inappropriate skills and since they are discriminated against both before and after they apply for their first job, they have great difficulty in finding an appropriate job or any job at all, with the result that occupational segregation persists. Not only is this disadvantageous for women themselves, but also for their children and for development in general. An ever-increasing number of families in the world are headed by women, most of whom are poor. In addition to these households depending solely on the income of women, many other families need the income of women in order to survive. As women's level of education and vocational training affects their job and income opportunities, and thus the standard of living of themselves and their families, it is essential that they be provided with the same access to training and employment as men. (van Ginneker 1986, 7)

Housing: The Right to Shelter

Housing needs are, as well, indicators of a serious structural impediment to economic and social justice deeply affecting women. The urban poor woman and her family have demonstrated the disastrous economic and social consequences of the global economic crisis and the inability of nations to meet basic housing needs while the military continues to consume vast resources.

Homeless single women are common in most major cities and have been especially noted in North America. Homeless families are everywhere, and orphaned or abandoned "street children" are among the most tragic homeless in the cities of Latin America and the rest of the developing world. The phenomenon of street children is a major indicator of the poverty and desperation of women who lack or lose the capacity to care for them. Poverty among men certainly affects families, but among women it is a cause of crisis that will affect the world and the possibilities for peace for generations to come. So great is this problem of street children that it was the subject of a report by the Independent Commission on International Humanitarian Issues. The prologue of the report paints a vivid and heart-wrenching picture.

An immense problem, with dramatic and unpredictable consequences, is emerging around the world:

Millions of 'street children' who live alone, undernourished since birth;
who are denied affection, education and help;
who live without love . . . .

As the big cities grow, so will the number of street children. So will deprivation which begets frustration which begets violence.

Both developed and developing countries face the problem without adequately addressing it.

The street is the common heritage of millions even before they are tainted by drugs, prostitution and crime.

We seek for these children the right to live a life worth living. (Independent Commission 1986, p. ii)

Problems of homelessness were also explored in a symposium, "Housing and Economic Development, a Women's Perspective," organized by the Conference on Non-Governmental Organizations in Consultative Status with UN/ECOSOC (Economics and Social Council) as a contribution to the Nairobi Conference (1985) and the International Year of Shelter for the Homeless (1987). One of the major points of the report clearly illustrates poor, urban women's special problems in regard to housing:

The impact of shelter solutions on women has always been great, due to the major role that women typically play in managing the household. But it is only recently that development planners have begun to focus at all on the potential differential impact of housing projects on women versus men and the particular housing and shelter needs that urban women may have. The importance of a women's perspective on housing and urban services has been underscored by the realization of women's substantial responsibilities for the economic well being of the household, the relevance of household location to women's employment opportunities, and the opportunity costs of women's time spent in obtaining urban services and participating in mutual and self-help schemes. Documentation of the increasingly large proportion of urban women who are single, divorced, or widowed heads of household has also helped to bring the issue of women and housing to the forefront. (Women's Issues in Housing Projects 1988, 6)

Housing is one of the primary needs most affected by military spending, and, as illustrated in the foregoing extracts, poor women have an especially acute need for affordable housing. Whether obtained by purchase, membership in a cooperative, or rental, the financing of housing as recognized in *The Nairobi Forward Looking Strategies* is a major problem for urban women.

Housing credit schemes should be reviewed and women's direct access to housing construction and improvement credits secured. In this connection, programmes aimed at increasing the possibilities of sources of income for women should be promoted and existing legislation or administrative practices endangering women's ownership and tenancy rights should be revoked. (FLS, para. 211)

The figures and quotations cited in this chapter, while especially highlighting the structures and conditions that impede women's enjoyment of economic and social justice, are in fact a description of the lot of the world's poor. The advantaged of the world, including women, have easy access to food, housing, education, and health services. The poor, men and women alike, do not. Although these structures impact more heavily on women, as do most social and economic problems, they are an obstacle to the fulfillment of the human needs of all the poor and, thereby, to the realization of universal human rights, the true measure of authentic security for the vast majority of the Earth's peoples.

"Changes in social and economic structures should be promoted which would make possible the full equality of women" (FLS, para.

53). Structural constraints that perpetuate poverty and women's oppression must be transcended, not only for the sake of equity for women, but for all humanity for the sake of the realization of an economically and socially just, nonviolent world. The standards set forth in the International Convention on Economic, Social, and Cultural Rights are a blueprint for such a world. The rights enumerated in this convention are most severely obstructed by the structural constraints embedded in the militarism still voraciously consuming world resources. Military spending is an undeniable link between physical and structural violence.

Military Spending as Structural Violence

One of the main obstacles to the effective integration of women in the development process is . . . a continuing arms race[4] which now may spread to outer space. As a result, immense material and human resources needed for development are wasted. (FLS, para. 95)

Preparation for war is the source of much of the structural violence suffered by women, as is readily demonstrated by the consequences of military spending. Marking the International Year of Peace in 1986, the world's military expenditures hit an all-time high of $900 billion. And that 1986 total has subsequently been outstripped by annual global military expenditures of at least a trillion dollars, more than the total debt of the developing countries. Only a few months after some happily animated discussions of the "peace dividend," the hoped-for result of the end of the cold war, the United States House of Representatives in November 1991 passed the largest national military budget in history, $400 billion. The economic costs of these ever-increasing expenditures are difficult to measure, but regular assessments are made, and most notable among them is the annual report, *World Military and Social Expenditures* (WMSE), authored and published by Ruth Leger Sivard, an economist formerly with the United States Arms Control and Disarmament Agency.[5] Many believe that the conceptualization of this report was an example of feminine thinking about public issues, a mode of thinking that puts a human perspective on economic and social data.

Sivard, who uses statistics to demonstrate that these figures are truly "people with the tears wiped off," provides us with such facts as: "Arms imports of developing countries between 1975 and 1985 amounted to 40 percent of the increase in their foreign debt for that period"; "Third World Military expenditures in constant prices have increased six-fold since 1960, unemployment eight-fold"; "three governments in five spend more to guard their citizens against military attack than against all enemies of good health" (Sivard 1987, 5). John Kenneth Galbraith emphasized the special burden borne by developing countries. "The poor countries collectively spend a larger percentage of their gross national product on arms than do the rich; they import weapons in the range of $30bn a year . . . . The consequence . . . is enormous cost to the poorest of the world's people" (Galbraith 1987, 6). This statistical evidence confirms the assertion that military expenditures are a major contributing factor to structural violence.

World Military and Social Expenditures is widely distributed to universities and governments, but it also has had a significant effect on women's organizations and peace organizations. For example, the March 1987 issue of *Peace and Freedom,* published by the Women's International League for Peace and Freedom, U.S. Section, opened with the following message from the section's president, indicating the shock and concern with which women in the peace movement received this information.

> Ruth Leger Sivard's 1986 compilation of "World Military and Social Expenditures," and the consequence to the human condition, is devastating. In his introduction, Dr. Bernard Lown calls Sivard's work "the sad facts that document the hemorrhage of scarce and vital resources consumed by the ever-escalating arms race."
>
> A few of those facts:
>
> - The nuclear stockpile of over 60,000 warheads represents more than 1 million Hiroshimas and 2700 times the explosive energy used in World War II (when 38 million people died).
> - 1 billion people, or 1 in 5, live below the poverty line.
> - 1 billion are inadequately housed; 100 million have no shelter at all; 1 in 3 adults cannot read or write.
> - Since 1960, unemployment has increased fourfold in richer countries and eightfold in poorer countries.
> - 700 million, or more than the entire population of the Western Hemisphere, do not get enough food for active, healthy lives.
> - At the current level of arms spending, the average person spends 3-4 years of his/her working life to pay for it.
>
> And finally, from Dr. Lown: "Every three days, 120,000 children die unnecessarily—the very toll of casualties following the atomic

bombing of Hiroshima. Indeed, the children of the world are already living in the rubble of World War III." (Ivey 1987, p. 2)

Concerns such as these led the U.S. section of WILPF to issue *The Women's Budget* (1986), a carefully researched and argued case for alternative expenditures that shift military expenditures to the civilian sector to meet human needs.[6] *The Women's Budget* reflects how the specific costs of the arms race are best illustrated by what equivalents spent on arms might otherwise provide to U.S. citizens. It is part of a growing literature on economic conversion.

For years, women peace researchers and activists have noted what could be done globally to meet human needs with alternative public expenditures released from a reduced military budget. In 1976, when worldwide expenditures were a mere third of what they were a decade later, Ruth Sivard suggested the following possibilities if military expenditures were reduced by 5 percent of the $300 billion spent at that time, providing $15 billion for social purposes:

What could $15 billion do to reduce the world's vast social deficit? Here are some possibilities in the form of inter-national cooperative programs for peaceful purposes, and their estimated annual costs. Each is a significant addition to existing programs. Together they would represent a start on a formidable fund for peace.

$4 billion: For 200 million malnourished children, supplementary protein feeding to insure full brain development.

$3 billion: For poor countries on the edge of famine, increased agricultural investment to enlarge food production.

$3 billion: Expansion of primary schools, with the addition of 100 million new places for children not now attending school.

$2 billion: Emergency aid and a permanent international relief force to assist disaster-stricken countries.

$1.5 billion: World-wide program for prevention of dental decay by fluoridation.

$1.0 billion: Basic education for 25 million adults now illiterate.

$450 million: World-wide campaign to eradicate malaria.

$45 million: Iron supplement to protect 300 million children and women of childbearing ages against anemia.

$5 million: Vitamin supplement to protect 100 million children
1-5 years against blindness caused by Vitamin A deficiency.
(Sivard 1977, 19)

With expenditures in the 1990s exceeding a trillion dollars, the
total release of funds would be equally greater. While, unhappily,
inflation prevents buying power from being increased on the same
scale, there would still be a great reduction in human misery and
structural violence, were even such a limited reduction and alternative expenditures realized. Consider, for example, a statistic cited on
the Public Broadcasting System's McNeil-Lehrer television news
program by Linda Darling-Hammond, that the annual education budget
proposed in 1991 by the president of the United States was about the
amount spent for one day of "Desert Storm," the Persian Gulf War (18
April 1991). UNESCO cites similar findings in *Challenge*:

About US$50 billion will be needed over the decade to make sure
every child is attending primary school by the year 2000. The
annual cost by the mid 1990's is roughly equivalent to the
amount the world now devotes to military expenditure every two
days. (Literacy Means Survival 1990)

All of the foregoing equivalents, however, refer to immediate
costs and consequences. What needs also to be taken into account are
the long-term implications, not only for the people, particularly for
women and children, whose needs go unfulfilled, but for the society
and the economy itself. The continued "hemorrhage of scarce and vital
resources" into the military have, and will continue to have, an
extremely destructive effect on social infrastructures, communities,
the urban environment, productive capacity, and the quality of life,
especially those qualities for which women bear most of the responsibility, families, households, education, the aged, and children, reneg-
ing on our responsibilities to future generations.

Families suffering the stress of poverty, unemployment, ill-
nesses untended, and malnourished children cannot provide a strong
social base or bring up a generation of healthy, socially responsible
youth. Households often solely supported by women will have to
absorb and fulfill needs and services that the society cannot provide,
adding to family stress and the burden of women as sole providers and
caregivers of families throughout the world. Communities that cannot
provide health care and education for all their members do not provide
the bases of strong, self-sufficient nations. Cities with inadequate

public transportation and communications systems, plagued by un-employment and homelessness, cannot be centers of commerce and production on which healthy economies are based.

Perhaps no other long-range cost of the arms race will so affect the future quality of life than the lack of resources for education. On a worldwide basis, one child in three does not attend primary school, and only one in two is in secondary school (Sivard 1983, p. 11). Their situation casts a long shadow over development goals, and develop-ment is a foundation for peace. Education is a crucial factor in social, cultural, and economic development. In every aspect, the future quality of life of the next generation will be negatively affected by lack of education. The shadow falls as well over the future of the industrial countries. As military expenditures exceed those for education in these nations, the futures of their young and their productive capaci-ties are put at risk. The age of information and the rapid advance-ments in technology, as pointed out in a 1987 newspaper series, have already outstripped educational systems geared to the earlier indus-trial age (*The Crisis in Education* 1987).

All of these conditions mortgage the future to a concept of national security that gives priority to the military over the economic and social sectors of society and emphasizes present and possible conflicts rather than potential future cooperation. As violence against the future, all of these costs uncover a concept of security that repeatedly imposes avoidable harm to all human, social, and eco-nomic potential. Women have always been concerned with the future, the future for which they bring up their own children and the future they seek to make better for all children. Thus, the costs of war and war preparations in present and in future terms is a profoundly serious women's issue. Like most women's issues, however, it is a truly human issue that concerns both women and men, those who now inhabit this planet and those who will replace them, whose lives also will suffer serious damage if we cannot wrest the future from the grasp of a shortsighted inadequate security system based solely on military might.

The data regularly issued by Sivard, together with the informa-tion on arms spending from the Stockholm Peace Research Institute and the research into the relationships between disarmament and development conducted by the United Nations, makes painfully clear that the poverty of the world is due in some significant measure to militarism and the arms race. So long as the arms race continues, the world community is not likely to meet developmental goals that could offer a decent and humane quality of life to most of the Earth's peoples.

Such "military security" is bought at the cost of poverty and misery, and much of that cost is paid by women and future generations.

The irony of weapons development, relentlessly pursued in the name of security, is that on every count of the concepts and criteria for real human security outlined in chapter 1, it results in a deficit. Military expenditures, as clearly illustrated by WMSE, have contributed to worldwide militarization, which itself threatens the present and future well-being of the human family. The life-sustaining capacity of the planet is eroded consistently by the devastating environmental damage caused by weapons testing. Basic human needs are denied as resources in ever greater volume are poured into weapons development, a contrast sharply illustrated by *World Military and Social Expenditures*. Personal well-being is thwarted and human rights violated for many, especially the poor and undereducated, because of unemployment resulting from the capital-intensive nature of the weapons industry prospering in the name of "national security." A distorted security policy for decades based on "deterrence," a precarious balance of nuclear capacity between the superpowers and now apparently dependent on the constantly shifting conventional weapons balance[7] among all buyers and sellers in the worldwide arms trade (as painfully demonstrated by the Persian Gulf War), makes war more, rather than less, likely. As the arms trade grows at an ever-increasing pace, the world continues on all counts to be less and less economically secure, a condition not significantly different from what it was more than a decade ago at the height of the cold war.

> The hundreds of billions of dollars spent annually on the manufacture or improvement of weapons are a sombre and dramatic contrast to the war and poverty in which two-thirds of the world's population live. This colossal waste of resources is even more serious in that it diverts to military purposes not only material but also technical and human resources which are urgently needed for development in all countries, particularly in developing countries. (*Final Document* 1978, para. 16)

The Women's Decade goal of development, the major hope for overcoming global structural violence, can be realized only if governments agree to "allocate a portion of the resources released through disarmament for purposes of social-economic development with a view to bridging the gap between developed and developing countries" (*Final Document* 1984, para. 35, sec. iv). Thus, economic conversion is a significant women's issue. It is to structural violence what demilitarization is to armed violence. Demilitarization and economic conversion are two sides of the same coin in the currency of peace.

Economic Conversion:
Reversing Structural Violence

Current peace research argues that military security depends on disarmament, and economic security, on conversion and development. One of the most significant contributions in the whole field of disarmament, a UN document known as "the Thorsson Report" (named after the Swedish woman, Inge Thorsson, who presided over the commission that drafted it), made the irrefutable link between disarmament and development and demonstrated unequivocally the negative economic and social effects of arms spending on both industrial and developing countries.[8] While women, the poor, and the vulnerable suffer most, the quality of life for all in all parts of the world is reduced by arms spending. The Thorsson Report has made this as clear as have Ruth Leger Sivard's annual reports on military expenditures. These reports demonstrate, as shall be discussed in greater detail below, that women are making significant contributions to disarmament. The concepts and insights these women have brought to understanding the economics of arms expenditures demonstrate how urgently women's perspectives are needed in the field of disarmament. They also have given considerable impetus to the ongoing inquiry into the possibilities and consequences of economic conversion from military production to goods and services to meet human and social needs. Their goal is to push forward the development process as a means of reversing the ever-increasing structural violence and potential armed violence that plagues world society.

Although the causes of underdevelopment are varied and complex, and military spending accounts for only one of them, economic conversion has become an issue of central concern and interest to researchers, international organizations, and peace activists. If savings from disarmament are in fact going to be channeled into development, much research and planning will be required. Several experimental programs have already been launched, and considerable study, particularly on effects on employment, has been undertaken. The International Labor Office is involved in such studies and has produced several publications, including a major study kit, "Making the Connection: Disarmament, Development, and Economic Conversion."[9]

Clearly, such conversion would benefit women, but more especially it would contribute to security, in that it would encourage other processes of demilitarization while making it possible to better meet a broad range of economic needs—if, for example, complemented by a shift from national self-defense to international peacekeeping and dispute settlement, it would significantly reduce the need for arms spending while reducing as well the likelihood of armed conflict between nations. Although we focus for the moment on the issue of economic conversion, this would be only one component of several interrelated processes and structural changes, sometimes referred to as "alternative security systems," directed toward strengthening the authentic global security women are seeking to achieve. Toward this end, economic conversion, in addition to being geared to disarmament and development, would have to be accompanied by confidence– building measures, effective dispute settlement procedures, and proposals for international peacekeeping. In mid 1992 the Secretary General issued a report with a set of recommendations for these purposes (Boutros Ghali 1992). However, economic conversion itself would be a significant step toward that goal.

Women's health needs will be better served by biological and scientific research concerned with such objectives as the development of nutrition supplements and safe methods of family planning rather than improving capacities in chemical and biological warfare. The construction of housing, schools, and health care centers in place of bombers and aircraft carriers will better serve the health and well-being of the whole society. Such production will be far less costly as well as provide more numerous and varied employment opportunities for both men and women. Many of the annual reports, *World Military and Social Expenditures,* as noted earlier, spell out in detail what specific benefits in terms of public health and social welfare could be gained by the reduction of military expenditures—thousands housed for the cost of a bomber, thousands more educated for the cost of a missile. Technology turned to the enhancement, rather than the destruction, of life will make for a more humane society, one characterized by feminine as well as masculine values. When the claim is made that there are vital relationships among disarmament, development, and security, women understand that such security is the fuller and broader authentic security that they know cannot be achieved without economic conversion and without a massive reallocation of resources from arms to development, from preparing for war to preparing for peace. As equality, development, and peace are inseparably interrelated, so too "peace, security, and economic and social development are indivisible" (*Final Document,* 1978). Economic conversion could overcome the structural violence endured by women. It is the one step that most clearly recognizes the indivisibility of peace, economic well-being, and security.

Realizing these connections has empowered many, especially women, to take direct action for social justice and against structural violence in such movements as Jobs with Peace (see appendix 4 for address).

Begun in 1978, Jobs with Peace is a national campaign that seeks to reorder our nation's priorities away from excessive military spending towards urgent human and environmental needs.

Jobs with Peace supports efforts towards the elimination of nuclear weapons, waste and fraud, and foreign intervention. We build grassroots organizations in low-income neighborhoods and communities of color to take leadership in efforts to challenge U.S. foreign policy—and to redirect our federal tax dollars to housing, health care, education, the environment and other socially useful enterprises. (Jobs with Peace 1991, 6)

Carla Jones of Milwaukee is an inspiration and example of how women are making the kinds of changes that can produce conversion, peace, and equity.

Never one to accept the status quo, Carla had a habit of confronting problems head-on. For example, in 1987, when the Milwaukee Housing Authority announced that 62 units in her development would be evacuated for lead paint removal, Carla began asking questions. Where would people go in the mean time? What guarantee was there they could return to their original homes? And if the lead problem was so bad, why had they been living with it so long? . . .

Carla would soon learn that Milwaukee Jobs With Peace wanted to organize a group of leaders to represent public housing tenants in all of the 5,000 units in the city. These residents had so many issues in common, it only made sense to join forces to empower themselves. Ann Wilson invited Carla to be a part of weekly meetings at the Jobs With Peace office to lay the plans for such an organization.

In November 1989, after two years of work, these planners hosted the founding convention for the Citywide Public Housing Residents Council. The convention was attended by 300 residents, who elected delegates to represent their respective housing develop-ments. The delegates in turn elected a Resident Council of 22 people who would go back to their various housing sites to survey resident concerns for the next meeting. Carla Jones was voted Treasurer . . . .

Carla took national Jobs With Peace events like Tax Day very seriously, realizing that Congress' spending of 50 cents of every tax dollar on the military and only 2 cents on housing would "eventually affect all of us right down the line—including people in public housing." She did door to door voter registration in her development and ran voter registration tables at outdoor festi-vals. And she made it a family affair. "I take my kids to all the rallies," says Carla. "They can talk about the savings and loan crisis as well as the Persian Gulf." Nevertheless, Carla empha-sizes, political activism begins at home. Says she, "People must first gain the confidence that they can affect their own lives at the grassroots level. (Jobs with Peace 1991, 8)

Positive peace is most likely to result from these kinds of efforts, individuals taking action at the local level to make the many specific changes that comprise economic conversion and economic development. As in all such community and global efforts, women are leading the way. They are leading in new theoretical and conceptual approaches, as is Rosalie Bertell; in networking and interacting with the United Nations, as in the Campaign against Gender Violence initiated by Charlotte Bunch; and meeting needs in their own communities, as is Carla Jones. The women's peace movement is about making connections and taking actions for a more secure world. Women are making connections among problems, such as the militarism-famine-environment links, and among organizations and movements from all over the world, such as those who met in Nairobi at the end of the International Women's Decade and in Miami to prepare for the United Nations Conference on Environment and Development. From such meetings have come actions that are changing world politics.

For Reflection and Discussion

1. How might you articulate a vision of global security based on economic and social justice and nonviolence? How would you use human rights standards to describe that vision?

2. How can the situation of women in regard to health, education, and employment reveal the general health of an economy? Why is the condition of women so significant a factor in the general welfare of entire populations?

3. How do the education, health, and employment gaps between men and women affect women's participation in public life? How can these effects be seen as structural constraints?

4. Are there hunger problems in your community? Are there efforts toward local food security? To what extent is that involvement affected by the roles of women? How might changes in the roles of women in your area and/or the policies of your country help in achieving global food security? What other problems stand in the way of food security? How do these problems affect this nation and others? How are these problems related to the roles and status of women?

5. What social values are reflected in the plight of the street children and the homeless? How might more public participation by women affect such values? Do the records of women in politics attest to your opinion on the matter?

6. What is the position of this nation and/or world region in global economic structures? What kinds of changes in those structures would best serve the interests of global security? How would the specific interests of each area of the world be affected by the changes you advocate? How would women's position be affected by such changes?

7. What effects on the struggle for peace and security might result from integrating women's rights into the current human rights paradigm?

For Reading and Further Study

Angela Davis. 1981. *Women, race, and class*. New York: Random House. Marxist analysis of women's position in the class structure of modern capitalist society.

Kate Millet. 1976. *Sexual politics*. New York: Doubleday. Analysis of the portrayal of the position of women in Western thought and literature, emphasizing the author's politicizing of gender.

Georgina Ashworth. 1986. *Of violence and violation: Women and human rights*. London: Change. Presents violence against women as a global human rights issue.

Audrey Bronstein. 1982. *The triple struggle: Latin American peasant women*. Boston: South End Press. Outlines the three layers of oppression suffered by rural poor women in developing countries.

Charlotte Bunch and Roxanna Carrillo. 1991. *Gender violence, a development and human rights issue*. New Brunswick, N.J.: Center for Women's Global Leadership. Argues that women's rights must become integral to conceptualization, and analysis of, and action for, the realization of universal human rights.

Myra Buvinic and S.W. Yudelman. 1989. *Women, poverty, and progress in the third world*. New York: Foreign Policy Association. A women's perspective on issues of economic development.

Barbara Ehrenreich and Annette Fuentes. 1983. *Women in the global factory*. New York: South End Press. Documents the gross exploitation of women by the international industrial system.

Kevin J. Cassidy. 1992. *Real security: Converting the defense economy and buildiing peace*. Albany: State University of New York Press. Provides evidence and analysis of how conversion from military to civil sector production can contribute to economic and social well-being.

Gail P. Kelly and Carolyn Elliott. 1982. *Women's education in the third world: Comparative perspectives*. Albany: State University of New York Press. Describes the educational deprivation and discrimination suffered by women in developing countries.

Seymour Melman. 1988. *The demilitarized society*. Montreal: Harvest House. Demonstrates the links between peace, disarmament and economic conversion.

June Nash. 1983. *Women and men in the international division of labor*. Albany: State University of New York Press. An analysis of how the world economic system exploits and contributes to women's depressed economic status.

Barbara Rogers. 1981. *The domestication of women*. New York: Methuen. Shows how the notion that women's sphere is the home has impeded development policy and perpetuates the poverty of women.

Four

Women's Roles in the Politics and Conceptualization of Peace

It is evident that women all over the world have manifested their love for peace and their wish to play a greater role in international cooperation, amity and peace among nations.

— FLS Para. 234

Peace: An Historical Concern of Women

Lysistrata, one of the great literary works of ancient Greece, although it is drama rather than chronicle, attests to women's long history of struggling for peace since ancient days when warring patriarchal tribes replaced the more egalitarian societies that first populated the European land mass (Spretnak 1983). In the centuries since then, women, not only in Europe but in all parts of the world, accepting their role in a patriarchal society, have also given support to war in many ways. As pointed out earlier, they have raised their sons to be warriors and their daughters to honor the warriors, and taught both to support the states that wage war. In fact, support of what most women believed to be a just and necessary war delayed and divided the women's suffrage movement in the early twentieth century.

. . . As in the Civil War, the Franco-Prussian wars and the Spanish-American War, the onset of World War I again curbed the rapid gains being made toward universal suffrage. But a number of U.S. women kept suffrage in the papers between the war news by an acceleration of tactics, including hunger strikes and the first protest demonstration at the White House. The demonstrators were arrested and imprisoned. Those on hunger strikes were painfully force fed.

In Canada (except for Quebec) women were successful in winning suffrage in 1917, despite the war. In general, though, most women felt the best they could do was hold the women's movement together until the war was over. In fact, many suffragettes turned their energies from "women's concerns" to the war. In England, for example, where suffragettes had been militant in efforts to keep their cause prominently before legislators and the public, they now ceased suffrage activity and devoted their organizational energies to folding bandages, working in hospitals and otherwise contributing to the war effort and national survival.

In the emotional heat of national mobilization, some women feared the cause of suffrage would be hurt by continued identification with work for peace. Reluctantly, those women wanting to continue work for peace—and especially to stop the war—continued suffrage work, but formed separate organizations for their peace initiatives. The Women's Peace Party was thus formed by women from Europe and North America. Its members convened two world congresses at the Hague in 1915 and 1919—with the objectives of stopping the war and preventing future wars. (Mische 1978, 2–3)

Not until the last quarter of the century were the cause of women and the cause of world peace seen as inseparable. Much of the foregoing in this book serves to illustrate that relationship. Yet, as we strive to integrate women's efforts, values, and visions of global security and viable peace into the larger struggle for world peace, we must keep in mind the histories of women's support of war, women's campaigns for their own rights, as well as women's struggle for peace. Elise Boulding, (1977), in a chapter "Women and Peace Work," helps us to place that struggle in a general historical context and to see how visions of a humane world have always informed it.

The new internationalism. Between 1820 and 1830, the first all-women national peace societies were founded in England and America, and by 1852 the Olive Leaf Circles were issuing the first international women's publication, *Sisterly Voices.* Women were also involved in the birth of the international labor movement. In 1840 the French-Peruvian, Flora Tristan Moscosa, at home on two continents, traveled around the world promoting her plan for a world-wide workers' international. Her plan was spelled out in her book, *L'Union Ouvriere*, published in 1843. The first Voix des Femmes, predecessor of the Canadian peace organization of that name formed in the 1960s, was born as a socialist movement in Paris in the 1840s. By the time of the establishment of the short-lived Paris Commune in 1871 many women had apprenticed themselves to the new internationalism. When Louise Michel broke into the bakeries of Lyons in 1882 to redistribute bread to the poor, she was bridging the gap between the housewives who rioted for bread in the 1700s, and the creators of the new socialist-anarchist vision of a post-imperial society. By the 1880s and 1890s, the vision of an international socialist community based on nonviolence and the repudiation of nationalism was being articulated by Clara Zetkin and Rosa Luxembourg . . . .

Groups of women sprang up all over Europe throughout the second half of the nineteenth century, women moving to a different rhythm from that of the military drumbeats to be heard everywhere . . . . Priscilla Peckover, an English Quaker, built up an international network of women with members in France, the Rhineland, Hanover, Rome, Warsaw, Connstantinople, Russia, Japan, Polynesia, Portugal, and the United States. (Stanton, 1970; Posthumus-van der Goot, 1961)

Austrian Bertha Sutner, author of one of the century's major works on disarmament, *Die Waffen Bieder* (Down with Arms, 1894), persuaded Alfred Nobel to found a peace prize. Jane Addams of the United States helped convene a group of women at the Hague during World War I, a group which would continue and would provide both the moral conscience and the scholarly know-how to create alternative institutions to war as an instrument of national diplomacy. Frances Willard, also of the United States, was an eloquent spokesperson for the new world view of women:

> We are a world republic of women—without distinction of race or color, who recognize no sectarianism in politics, no sex in citizenship. Each of us is as much a part of the world's union as is any other woman; it is our great, growing, beautiful home [Gordon, 1924; 69].

These women were responding to an intricate complex of issues; war, slavery, economic injustice, and the misery of the urban poor were all on their agendas. The women's rights movement

developed almost incidentally, as women found civic problem-
solving roles closed to them because of their sex. The new
internationalism for women was not simply an extension of the
older roles of creating public structures of nurturance. Something
else was going on, a reconceptualization of social structures and
social roles. Women were beginning to recognize their complicity in
war and social injustice. They saw that their acceptance of
traditional underside nurturance roles made the war business
easier for men. Even the Florence Nightingales became politicized,
and men fought against the new civic roles for women because they
feared the changes that would follow . . . .

By the early 1900s, we are struck with the high degree of
professionalization and commitment to public life of the women in
these international movements . . . . Between 1900 and 1915
the first three women's organizations focused primarily on international relations were born, as were five new inter-national religious
associations for women. By 1930 three more international relations groups and ten organizations for professionally specialized
women had been born. All of these groups, and also the international educational associations for women founded before and after
1900, had international peace as one of their primary concerns. The
international relations associations are distinct from the other
groups, however, in that they focused primarily on the political
institutions and processes of peace and war . . . .

There is something of a hiatus between the women's peace movement as it took shape in the early part of this century and the
movements involving women activists today. The professional
tradition of that earlier generation of women was buried in the
back-to-the-home movement of the thirties and forties, so well
described by Betty Friedan in *The Feminine Mystique* (1963). The
six international relations organizations active before the thirties,
and the four born since then, are all very much alive, but their
organizational role is not as clear as in the earlier period. There has
always been a Lysistrata component in their activities—protest
and noncompliance. The public structures-of-nurturance component has also continued, for no women's organization has been
willing to ignore the social suffering of the deprived. But the work
of reconceptualization of society as a global system begun by
women in the last century has slowed down somewhat. We will
see . . . in the following pages on women as scholars, activists,
national and international public officials, and military person-

nel that few women have a significant opportunity to affect world peace potentials in any of these roles. (Boulding 1977, 167–73,)

The growing emphasis on women's history, as these excerpts, from Boulding indicate, points to women's active roles in preventing and ending hostilities, as hostages married into opposing camps, as informal negotiators, and in some instances as translators and representatives. In the nineteenth century, women suffragists advocated settling disputes through law and arbitration. Women in the early decades of this century struggled to prevent war, taking an even stronger and more deliberate role, though that role still remains for the most part outside the formal structures of power. The women described by Boulding are today a significant source of inspiration to women peace activists. Jeannette Rankin, whose efforts to avoid World War I contributed to the foundation of the Women's International League for Peace and Freedom (WILPF), has been honored by the United States Institute of Peace in naming its library for her. These efforts, however, cost Jeannette Rankin her seat in the U.S. Congress and Emily Greene Balch, another WILPF founder, her position at Wellesley College. Indeed, women's priority for peace and justice, their struggles for the ameliorization of conditions of poverty, the abolition of slavery, and the avoidance of war often have been at the expense of their own rights. World War I was not a unique case in this regard. In earlier years, as indicated by Mische, women more often acquiesced to the separation and prioritizing of issues. American women, Abigail Adams notwithstanding, deferred equality to the task of gaining acceptance for the newly crafted federal constitution of 1789. While Sojourner Truth from the experience of slavery drew a vivid picture of the capacity of women to do "men's work," her white sisters placed abolition above women's suffrage, just as their daughters and granddaughters were to place victory in war. The traditional women's peace movement tended to focus primarily on war and international conflict. However, in recent years, an unshakable insistence on the feminist tendency to interrelate the central problems and pursue holistic strategies of resolution characterizes large segments of the movement. Yet beneath the urgent efforts to prevent or end the outbreak of hostilities, women were always preoccupied by the underlying causes and the problems of economic and social justice as well as issues of political freedom for individuals and nations.

Until more recent decades, women's peace work has been carried out mainly through the nongovernmental structures described in

Women in the Twentieth Century World (Boulding 1977). These organizations in the first half of the century were for the most part made up of women from the industrial countries, primarily the United States and Western Europe. However, in the years since World War II and the founding of the United Nations, women have developed a truly planetary perspective on the human condition. As the traditional women's peace organizations began to globalize their memberships, members developed a sophisticated global analysis of the interrelationship among world problems. They perceived their task as helping others to see the world as a whole, the peoples of the Earth as one family, and to understand that at the core of most world problems were the unchecked forces of violence—in Boulding's terms, behavioral violence, or, in the terms used here, both physical and structural violence, whether personal, domestic within the home, or international violence in the warfare that constantly ripped the delicate fabric of human society.

Women began to see how the policies of the industrial nations affected people's quality of life, particularly in the developing nations, and how this global interdependence characterized every aspect of our personal and local experience. The UN Decade for Women was both a reflection and an instrument of global interdependence. As women from developing countries entered into dialogue with those from industrialized countries, the pattern of interrelationships that ultimately brought forth the three themes of the Decade for Women emerged. Even before the Nairobi conference stated the undeniable relationships among equality, development, and peace, some sectors of the women's peace movement had incorporated these interrelationships into their analyses, actions, and programs, as the feminine perspective tends to do. This recent history points to a women's global framework that manifests the holistic feminine view of the world and of the human condition.

A holistic view attends as much to the local and the personal as it does to the global and the political, and acknowledges the interconnections, or the "continuum of violence." Indeed, women have come to understand global issues and problems of peace and war most profoundly by seeing how they affect their own daily lives and those of their families and neighbors. A son called up for military service has led many to an analysis of militarism; the loss of one's own or a spouse's job has led to a reflection on the world economy and military spending. As more women have experienced these problems personally and analyzed them locally within a global context, they have devised multilevel approaches to their resolution, the "reconceptualization of society as a global system" that Boulding recounts as characteristic of women's internationalism in the nineteenth century.

This multilevel, transnationalist global approach to local and regional actions for peace and justice has become a pronounced characteristic of the contemporary women's peace movement. Profound and significant changes are taking place at the local level throughout the world. These changes are often impelled by the recognition of the need to eliminate the source of militarism and the remains of colonialism, and to extend and invigorate the struggle against sexism, racism, apartheid, and all forms of foreign domination. New grassroots organizations and less formal movements have sprung up all over the world, involving millions in global efforts for peace and justice. Women within official governmental structures, formal nongovernmental organizations, people's movements, and grassroots actions constitute a new source of energy for the peace movement. Women from areas of regional conflict speaking out against armed intervention, women hugging trees to prevent the deforestation of Asia, mothers demonstrating against torture and disappearance in Latin America, nuns kneeling before tanks to prevent violence against people struggling for their liberation from dictatorships, women enduring their own and their husbands' imprisonment for actions against apartheid, women of all ages marching against nuclear weapons, all are part of this great surge of feminine energy for peace and life.

Women's energy was manifested by the thousands who came to Nairobi in 1985 to observe the formal end of the Women's Decade. It was most vividly demonstrated in the Peace Tent, the heart of the nongovernmental forum, where the women's global peace ethic was put into practical operation. The mass of energy and action for the evolving causes of women and peace emerged at Nairobi, serving as clear evidence of a beginning, of a new, purposeful, and vigorous women's movement for justice and peace. This movement is well characterized in Hilkka Pietila's paper, "Women's Peace Movement as an Innovative Proponent of the Peace Movement as a Whole." In her conclusion, she provides some significant insights into women's perspectives on the issues of war and violence and the need for these perspectives in reaching a deeper, more adequate analysis of the problems.

I already noted in the beginning, that it is impossible to separate the women's movement from the women's peace movement. The feminist movement is a peace movement, because it aims at building such a realm of values and way of life where violence, oppression and inequality would be minimized. Thus, the women's peace movement means building a world of peace and bringing up peaceful human beings rather than struggling against the arms race, authoritarianism and militarism.

Developments in the world in recent years and the efforts by governments so far have shown that men themselves are power-less and perplexed with their own violence and their systems of violence. Without new measures men's institutions of power seem to have no idea—let alone means—of how to break out of this vicious cycle.

From women's point of view, the most important "defence force" is the one which would help them defend themselves against the violence of men's world, always and everywhere. But the situation must not, however, be developed into a battle between men and women or between men's and women's realms of values. That would only mean drawing the front line of men's mutual fight and competition between the two sexes, too. This would not contribute to promoting equality and decreasing violence.

But instead, it has to be possible to analyze honestly and without prejudices the cultural norms and sexual myths underlying the present ideal of being a male, men's need of performance, competition and desire for power and the structures established for carrying out all this. It is easier for women to carry out this analysis because they are not so "challengeable" as men are. Women have less [investment in] these myths and values, although they themselves may also be confused by their vested interest to rid themselves of "the role of the victim and object" and to become an equal partner.

The success of this analysis is in the interest of men as well as women. Therefore it only can be wished for that there is enough maturity among men so that they could accept the results of the analysis made by the women's movement. For their own part, men should respond to the process and set themselves out to an equally unprejudiced analysis of their own culture and try to get rid of their own "masculine mystique." The interaction of these processes and the combined utilization of the results is a way which might lead out of the present impasse. (Pietila 1987, 4)

Women's Participation in Decision Making
Related to Peace and Security

> Women should participate fully in all efforts to strengthen and
> maintain international peace and security. . . . The commit-
> ment to remove the obstacles to women's participation in the
> promotion of peace should be strengthened. (FLS, para. 240)

While it is clear that women have a right to participate in public
policy-making for peace and that their perspectives and approaches are
sorely needed, the reality of their actual roles in the political fora where
policies are made is made poignantly clear in the powerful statement by
Joanne Woodward, chairperson of the U.S. National Women's Conference to Prevent Nuclear War held in Washington in 1986.

> Women were never consulted about the need for 50,000 nuclear
> warheads and women have no need to defend the decisions that
> produced them. Women have no vested interest in protecting or
> maintaining the status quo of military policies because they
> played no role in developing those policies. (Woodward 1986)

Women's involvement in the formal governmental and
intergovernmental processes has not increased significantly since a
publication prepared by UNESCO for the 1980 Copenhagen conference. The opening statement of an article on the subject carried by the
publication is still valid today: "In spite of much discussion and
exhortation, women continue to be chronically under represented in
international decision making" (McLean 1980, 54). The absence of
women in international decision making and peace processes is
directly related to their absence from the highest levels of national
decision making, the level at which the most significant decisions on
issues of peace and security are currently taken. During the entire
International Women's Decade, there was, according to a 1985 report
by the Inter-Parliamentary Union, less than a 2 percent increase in
women representatives in parliamentary assemblies (Inter–Parliamentary Union 1985).

Although few nations deny women the right to vote, few also
have had women national leaders. Nor have most of those few women
who have attained the highest office in their nations made any visible
effort to appoint more women to cabinet level positions or to positions
related to security policy. (The few women who have served in such
positions have made outstanding contributions in virtually every

field, including disarmament.) Gerald Mische has attributed this to the structural and systems constraints on all heads of state, including women leaders (Mische 1986). They, too, are bound by the "national security straitjacket" and by the international system of competitive "sovereign" states.

In the United Nations, women also have been sorely underrepresented. Within the organization, some women have formed the Group on Equal Rights for Women, with the purpose of assuring that there will be "no restrictions on the eligibility of men and women to participate in any capacity and under conditions of equality in its principal and subsidiary organs" (The Charter of the United Nations, art. 8). In their periodical, *Equal Time*, they reported on women's struggle for equality within the UN. Their special issue for the UN's fortieth anniversary highlighted the major contributions women have made to the organization, showing that since the UN's formation, a few women have been among the most visible and significant actors on the UN scene. The work of most women in the UN, they charged, went unacknowledged. They cited "uncontestable" evidence.

The directory of "senior officials" of the organizations and agencies of the United Nations system published in March, 1985, by the UN Office of Secretariat Services for economic and social matters. For those of us in the ad hoc group who monitor the progress in women's participation in the running of the world body, it demonstrates that the decade for women has been a failure above all where it was supposed most to obtain leadership and moral example. With nothing to celebrate this 40th Anniversary of Article 8 of the UN Charter, we dedicate this whole issue to the countless invisible numbers of women who have put their minds and energies into keeping the United Nations system running smoothly over 40 years of little recognition and constant discrimination against them: the women who work throughout the system as technical and secretarial support, communication and language services, conference facilitators, medical units of staff, and maintenance, elevator and cleaning services.

Women are especially underrepresented at the higher levels of the professional categories. To take into account the differences among the various grade levels when measuring the representation of Member States, a system was devised by which each grade level is weighted according to the gross salary at step one of each grade. (In the statistics provided to the General Assembly—

which do not include a breakdown by sex—other factors, such as population, are included in the calculations by which a weighted figure is arrived at. These figures are not officially used in setting recruitment guidelines, etc.).

Measured strictly in terms of numbers, the proportion of women in posts subject to geographical distribution is 23.1 percent as of June 1985; an improvement over last year, but still short of the 25 percent target established by the General Assembly ten years ago. However, when the representation of women is looked at in terms of the levels at which they are represented, by assigning the appropriate weight for each grade, a more accurate and revealing picture emerges. The weighted proportion of women in the professional categories is 19.2 percent as opposed to 80.8 percent for men, and the official figure of 23.1 percent.

Calculation of Weighted Representation of Women
Reference: A/40/65

Grade	Weight of Grade	No. of F Staff	Weighted Representation	No. of M Staff	Weighted Representation
USG	96.8	—	0	27	2,613.6
ASG	85.9	4	343.6	26	2,233.4
D-2	67	3	201.00	88	5,896.00
D-1	55.9	22	1,229.8	237	13,248.3
P-5	48.7	43	2.094.1	532	25,908.4
P-4	38.2	166	6,341.2	657	25,097.4
P-3	30.5	260	7,930.0	549	16,744.5
P-2	24.2	199	4,815.8	254	6,146.8
P-1	18.2	19	345.8	16	291.2
Total weighted representation:			98,179.6		23,301.3
			19.2%		80.8%

(*Equal Time* 1985, 1)

To this very day, the overall position of women in the world body continues to be one of shocking underrepresentation.

In May 1990, the UN Economic and Social Council adopted resolutions requesting the Secretary General to take steps to ensure that 35 percent of UN professional posts would be held by women and urging governments to work for more political participation and representation of women. A previous goal of 30 percent of the secretarial posts for women by 1990 was not met. In December 1989, the figure was 27.2 percent. There were two under-secretaries general and no woman assistant secretary general. At the beginning of 1991, there were only four women who headed agencies. In November 1992, in a welcome surprise announcement the Secretary General announced a goal of 50 percent representation of women in the Secretariat.

As women have thus far been so woefully underrepresented in the Secretariat and specialized agencies, so, too, women have seldom served as heads of delegations; only two have sat on the Security Council, and women have been equally represented in only a few delegations. Only two women have served as presidents of the General Assembly, a third ran and lost. Yet women have carried the important tasks of the clerical and secretarial work that is absolutely essential not only to the Secretariat but to the day-to-day work of the specialized agencies of the UN—the core work that touches people's lives and demonstrates what the organization can do, and is doing, for a more just and less violent world.

Insights into overcoming impediments to women's involvement in international organizations and decision making are revealed in a paper prepared by Elise Boulding for an experts' meeting on the topic organized by the UN Branch for the Advancement of Women in 1983.

> Surveying the preconditions for women's involvement in peace-related decision-making we have seen that in spite of legal commitments to equality of participation much has yet to be done to involve women in decision-making in political, economic, and social affairs at the national level in order to prepare the pool of women's expertise needed for policy inputs in international affairs. At the same time, looking at the record of women's representation in local and national bodies, and in international roles at the UN, as well as in nongovernmental roles, one gets the distinct impression that there is a very large pool of experienced and competent women pushing at the doors of every opportunity. Yet social custom and political experience keep those opportunity doors shut. Progress is uneven, and very slow.

> One strategy for the next women's decade might be to focus on all the unusual peacemaking and peacekeeping skills women have developed, and to campaign to place those skills where they are most needed. Three specific targets should be considered: (1) representation of one-third women on all national security bodies and all international security bodies including NATO and the Warsaw Pact, (2) women's units in the UN Expeditionary Forces, and (3) special UN women's peace brigades for dealing with civil violence. Equivalent national brigdes

could also be considered. For the non-governmental sphere, some goals might be: (1) women's encampments at all international borders where violent combat is in process of being threatened, consisting of women trained in nonviolence;[1] (2) travelling teams of women mediators sponsored by women's organizations; (3) a special program of recruitment of young women to study international affairs, conflict resolution, and mediation, with scholarship support for such training. Such programs would help make women's contributions to peacemaking more visible and accessible.

The diversity among women of ways of analyzing the problems of stimulating peace processes in a highly armed world, and the diversity of strategies chosen, should be taken as an asset and not as a handicap. Decision-making is not a simple one-dimensional process organized in clearcut structures with identifiable key access points. It is a diffuse process that goes on at many levels and with many access points, from that of kindergarten rooms where conflict resolution is being taught to five-year-old boys and girls to the national security council meetings in top-secret closed sessions which decide on weapons deployment. The task of women is to introduce alternative strategies at every decision point they can manage to touch, public and private. Always women must seek to expand the number of settings in which they can work, and the number of skills they bring to that work. (Boulding 1983)

Women have been bringing an expanded number of skills to many settings dealing with the most fundamental security issue, disarmament.

Women and Disarmament: On the Cutting Edge

Women have enhanced many of their analytic skills within the framework of United Nations efforts in disarmament. They have done this work mainly as members of the nongovernmental organizations through which citizen participation in the United Nations becomes ever more important. NGOs operate in all fields of UN action. Those associated with disarmament have been especially important.

As part of the preparatory activities for a conference on disarmament and development convened in 1987, the Secretary General convened "a panel of eminent personalities" to explore the issues in

April 1986. Sadly, only one woman was named to the fifteen-member panel; happily, that woman was Inge Thorsson, who again served as the chairperson of the panel. Two NGO committees at UN headquarters in New York, one on disarmament and one on development, took advantage of the convening of the panel to organize a public forum that included the contributions of a number of women. The focus was initiated and carried out by women from the NGO Disarmament Committee at UN headquarters. At UN headquarters in Geneva, too, women are the energizing force of the NGO community and take a leading and active part in disarmament affairs.

Women have also been active in bringing to public attention disarmament proposals for alternative security systems, among them the reconsideration of the concept of a standing United Nations peacekeeping force and the strengthening of all UN capacities for peacekeeping. Inquiries into such possibilities were conducted by NGO's long before the recommendations were issued by the Secretary General (Boutros-Ghali 1992).

Making the links between disarmament and development, as Thorsson and Sivard have done, is but one example of making connections between issues, a process that is constitutive of women's way of thinking in terms of interrelationships. Although the focus on this set of interrelationships has been sharpened and clarified and extended to include economic conversion, the links to women, women's oppression, and women's ways of thinking, none of these interconnections are yet sufficiently part of policy discourse.

Women have long been among the advocates of disarmament, as the sine qua non for the achievement of peace. Earlier in this century, in preparation for the 1930 European Conference on Disarmament, women collected nine million signatures on a petition urging serious reduction in naval forces, the most significant strategic factor at that time. Petitioning has been a major tool used by women in attempting to encourage disarmament. Indeed, while women have played a minor role in actual disarmament negotiations, they have been extremely active in lobbying the policymakers and participating in all and any activities open to them to influence the disarmament process.

It was women who aroused and organized the public in massive educational and petition campaigns in support of the Limited Test Ban Treaty of 1963. The late Josephine Pomerance, in whose honor the NGO Disarmament Committee at UN headquarters in New York presented awards for contributions to disarmament within the UN system, was a major organizer of such efforts. A new peace organization, Women's Strike for Peace, was organized to work for this and other disarmament measures. A woman, Randall Forsberg, conceived the Nuclear Freeze, and many other women joined her in making it a major international campaign. Women also inspired and organized the great public support for the Second Special Session on Disarmament in 1982 in one of the greatest peace demonstrations of history. Even during the cold war, U.S. and Soviet women together, convened conferences and discussed ways in which they could work together. The Soviet cosmonaut Valentina Tereshkova, the first woman in space, was a vigorously articulate spokesperson for peace and disarmament. Women throughout the world have been the main activists in grassroots consciousness–raising about the arms race and the arms trade. In 1970, Japanese women protested the militarization of Mt. Fuji with the Shibokusa Women's Peace Camp. In 1985, the International Women's Peace Camp in Geneva was reestablished to remind diplomats at the UN that women whose concerns for disarmament run deep and strong are still closed out of arms negotiations. Over the decade of the '80s, many women gave up five or more years of their lives to such encampments, most notably the brave women of Greenham Common, as witness of a truly courageous and steadfast commitment to disarmament. Though subject to ridicule, harrassment, sometimes physical harm, the Greenham women for many years continued their special witness for peace, against the United States deployment of nuclear weapons at this British military base.

Women professionals, workers, and housewives separately and together have held conferences to deepen their knowledge, offer each other support, and declare their hopes and visions to the world. A number of these have been international such, as the one held in Halifax, Nova Scotia, in June 1985, in Wisconsin in 1987, and Vanauatu in 1991. Women gathered to share their concerns and plan strategies for addressing them.

Women in government have held similar meetings and published similar statements. World Women Parliamentarians for Peace organized in 1985 mainly out of their concerns about the arms race and human survival. Their statement reflects a comprehensive, feminine view of peace.

For true equality to become a reality for women, the sharing of power on equal terms with men is vital. Women should fully participate in all efforts, including negotiations, to strengthen and maintain peace and to promote international cooperation, *detente* and nuclear and conventional disarmament. Governments must implement this by institutional, educational, and organizational changes . . . .

Urgent action is needed to halt the technological escalation of the conventional and nuclear arms race. To achieve this goal we recommend the reallocation of funds to non-military research and development, limits on international arms transfers in general, particularly to areas of conflict, and the conversion and redeployment of resources released from military purposes to economic and social aid to developing countries.

Men and women all over the world long for peace and justice. Interdependence between nations is greater than ever. Unfortunately, the search for security has too much been based on national aspirations and armaments, and too little on common efforts towards mutual understanding and international peace. It is our firm belief that this pattern has to be broken, if humankind is to survive. In the nuclear age, security must be based on common interests instead of confrontation and nuclear deterrence. The technological imperative of the arms race must be replaced by concrete political initiatives for disarmament.

In principle all nations and governments condemn the arms race, but in practice they participate in that race. The dilemma is to find ways of transition from one security system to a different one. As women parliamentarians we fully realize this difficulty, but we cannot accept the existing stalemate, which prevents progress in the necessary disarmament process.

We therefore *propose* these transitional measures: an immediate moratorium on the testing, production and deployment of nuclear weapons and their delivery vehicles, reciprocally undertaken by the Soviet Union and the United States followed by the other nuclear powers. We also *propose* negotiations aiming at formal agreements beginning with a comprehensive test ban treaty. We further *call* for the absolute prevention of an arms race in space. These actions constitute the foundation for agreements on sharp reductions of the immense arsenals of nuclear and conventional weapons.[2]

Unified in our concern for peace and disarmament and convinced that the arms race is a fundamental obstacle to peace, equality and development, we have formed *World Women Parliamentarians for Peace*. The compelling agenda of this network will be the implementation of these and other proposals at the national and international level.

> We invite women parliamentarians from all continents and political systems to join us in this urgent task. (Women's Parliamentarians' Statement 1985)

In Athens, in late 1986, a meeting was organized by Women for a Meaningful Summit (later to become Women for Mutual Security) that marked a high point in women's international cooperation for disarmament, by bringing their concerns directly to the negotiators themselves, often the heads of state. This meeting was facilitated by Margarita Papandreou, then first lady of Greece. At this meeting and a year later, in Moscow at an international women and peace conference organized by the Soviet Women's Committee and attended by three thousand women peace activists, and later in the United States, Papandreou offered a powerful message about the role of women in peacemaking.

> And just to make sure you don't consider me overly pro-woman, I want to tell you that I know many men who have the same goals— and we will welcome them—we will need them in this new adventure of women in public affairs. To the question, "Will it really make a difference?" I want to reply with a question. The Oxford Research Group in England has spent six years finding out in the two superpower countries, and in the other three main nuclear countries—France, England, China—where decisions are being made about nuclear armaments, research, control, etc. and by whom. They drew up a list of 800 people who are the decision-makers on this vital issue. Out of the 800, four are women. Now I ask you, if those figures were reversed, and there were 796 women and four men, wouldn't the decisions be different? I believe sincerely that they would. (Papandreou 1987)

Women also have made significant contributions to the disarmament process itself and to public understanding of the issues and problems involved in disarmament. In her book *The Game of Disarmament* (1978), the late Alva Myrdal, a Swedish arms negotiator, laid bare the fundamental ineffectiveness of years of negotiation in "arms talks." She observed that such talks failed to reduce arms and instead made many obsolete, opening the way to further development of more "sophisticated" weapons. Sheila Tobias, an American, in *The People's Guide to National Defense, What Kinds of Guns Are They Buying for Your Butter* (1984), broke through the mystique of weaponry and the jargon of weaponeers, making it possible for the average citizen and all women to understand technical aspects of the arms race we had been told only "experts" could deal with. Betty Lall, another American, in *Security without Star Wars* (1987), argued against the anti-ballistic missile system. In *How Nuclear Weapons Decisions Are Made* (1986), Scilla McLean (Elworthy) from the United Kingdom shed light on the process of nuclear weapons decision making and the need for public awareness and participation in the process.

Women, whether they are professional researchers and analysts or volunteer activists, bring to their activism and to their exposition of issues related to security a sophisticated knowledge that is the product of keeping well abreast of all developments, and while their numbers are few, those who are full-time peace researchers are becoming more influential.

Women in Peace Research: New Perspectives on the Fundamental Questions

If we define peace research as inquiry into the means and possibilities of reducing violence, abolishing war, and creating a just and equitable society, then it is clear from much of what already has been recounted here that women have been among the most active and productive peace researchers. They have been members of peace research institutes, university faculties, international organizations, professional associations, and such structures through which peace research is and has been conducted.

In some cases when the research questions most pertinent to a feminist perspective on peace and security were or could not be addressed within such structures, women founded their own institutes. The Institute for Training in Non-violence, set up by Beverly Woodward; the Institute for Defense and Disarmament, started by Randall Forsberg; World Priorities, founded by Ruth Sivard; and the Oxford Research Group, established by Scilla Elworthy[3] are all cases in point. Women have established, facilitated, and contributed to all the projects that have provided the basic knowledge we now have about war, militarism, the arms race, and the causes and possible solutions to the whole range of related global problems. As in other spheres of human activity, women's contributions have often been co-opted or ignored, and only a few women are recognized as leaders in the peace research field. These, however, are well-respected, first-rank researchers. Although considerable progress toward inclusion has been made, and in recent years more women are publishing their peace and security research (see appendix 5) some aspects of a critique of the field with regard to its exclusion of women and women's perspectives published in 1985 still prevail.

Both peace research and world order studies have been sorely lacking in the personal, the particularly human dimension of analysis and prescription. This is clearly evident in the minimal consideration given to women's issues and women's movements and in the failure heretofore to include sexism as a problem for research and analysis.

A more obvious and more serious exclusion is that of much of the relevant work women have done in peace research and of the participation of women themselves. Peace researchers, like other professioonals, are always hard put to think of more than one or two qualified women to participate in or contribute to any scholarly endeavor. Qualified, of course, means conforming to masculine standards of professional competence, that is, having passed the appropriate masculine success tests. So it is that few women, and fewer feminists, have been read or heard, much less attended to, in research and policy discourse. In the arms and militarization field this is especially lamentable, for nowhere are fresh views and new voices more urgently needed. (Reardon 1985, 71-72)

Elise Boulding, who conducted a survey in seventeen countries, reports some of women's particular contributions to disarmament research that are pushing outward the boundaries of the concepts and definitions of security.

Almost evey respondent proposed research on the concept of national security itself. Most scholars want questions to be asked about the political, economic and social conditions that would make disarmament possible, to replace the focus on technical curbs. There is widespread concern that research perspectives on disarmament are too Western: "War is still perceived as an outbreak in the European theatre." Arms trade is also viewed too much from a first world perspective, the respondents say, with too many assumptions about "valuable spinoffs" from the military for the Third World, and no solid research on "how militaries affect the allocation of resources within individual societies and thus shape the development strategy planned." A lack of research on militarization in neutral and non-aligned countries as a distinct type of phenomenon in the world militarization process is pointed out.

Many focus on the need to understand the contexts in which disarming processes can take place, and complain of our ignorance of the cultures of other States and regions . . . . Scholars study negotiation processes far too little, and pay little attention to developing models of peaceful settlement of conflict . . . .

In general, there is a call to move "away from the pseudo-scientific, pseudo-technical approach to arms control and concentrate on the issues that affect each of us . . . . It's not the response time of radar or the trajectory of ballistic missiles but the economic and social cost of military expenditures and the consequences of military solutions to political problems that matter." "I wish the research community would devote more resources to investigating *how* specific disarmament measures would function in the real world."

. . . Alva Myrdal, the scholar who has been in the disarmament field the longest, emphasizes in *The Game of Disarmament* the interrelationship between secrecy and militarization, and the importance of publishing Yearbooks detailing arms expenditures, military budgets and arms trade for every nation.[4] Many of the respondents in this study are in fact contributing to that kind of documentation. Their very immersion in such data has led them to call for contexts in which the data can be put, hypotheses and models that will organize information meaningfully. There can be no argument that both are needed. Myrdal's own primary concern is precisely for context . . . .

. . . "Our security can't be turned over to others. It is a state of mind." No one suggested that security depended on arms. Many agreed that absolute levels of destructive hardware pose more dangers than the risks of miltiary imbalances *vis-a-vis* other nations. Reducing present armed forces to the size of police forces with strong inhibitions as to their use was seen as a way to repair the concept of security in relation to military force. The general thrust of the comments was in the direction of developing problem-solving skills and communication skills to replace the use of force, and to redefine national security goals in the context of international security and well-being. New definitions of national identity, new awareness of a broader human identity and a reordering of value priorities which involves willingness to live with uncertainty are seen as involved. One respondent saw the development of human rights doctrines and policies as assisting in this process. (Boulding 1980)

The 1983 consultation of women peace researchers organized by the International Peace Research Association (IPRA) at Gyor, Hungary, on "Women, Militarism, and Disarmament," defined a "continuum of violence" (noted in chapter 2), and shed further light on feminist perspectives on violence and war, by identifying five areas of needed research. They called for increased research attention to sexism and sex-role socialization; the connections between sexism and other forms of discrimination and violence, and between militarism and development; the common characteristics of the feminist and peace movements; the connections between action and research; core concepts, root causes, and strategies for a change of values and consciousness, in order to understand better the effects of militarization, as well as direct violence, on women; and the role of women in promoting new understandings of war and peace.

Some of the explanatory comments contained in the report on this consultation highlight women's approaches to peace research.

We are both women and researchers and as such, we feel the agonies of individual human suffering and want, as Art. 3 of the IPRA Charter states, we seek "to advance interdisciplinary research into the conditions of peace and the causes of war and other forms of violence." Thus, as women from 13 countries in all regions of the world, we discussed research on the relationship between women, militarism and disarmament and the need for a praxis approach to conceptualizing the problems and the nature of our work. As some of our sisters came from Central America and South Africa we felt particular solidarity with all sisters in these areas who are especially the objects of violence and injustices of all sorts from their own governments and the violence of the militaristic international system. We want to express to IPRA not only our sense of empathy but our sense of responsibility for researching the root causes of all this violence and working actively towards just solutions . . . .

Seeing and hearing real people suffering violence in all of its forms, we propose to ourselves and to our male colleagues in IPRA that research on sexism and on its connections with other forms of violence, are an appropriate part of IPRA's research agenda. We propose that IPRA should officially acknowledge this by the creation of a study group which will formulate a feminist research agenda to address these questions and bring them to all the commissions. We encourage convenors of each commission to invite papers on concerns of special interest to women and encourage IPRA to recognise women researchers by appointing them as convenors as well. We see connections between our work as feminists and our work as peace researchers, and our feelings of humanity towards others who suffer. We urge all our colleagues in IPRA to recognise our concerns and the legitimacy of research on these connections. (IPRA 1983, 1)

Getting these issues on the broader peace research agenda continues to be a struggle for feminists in the field. They have sought to identify issues and problems for research. Earlier in 1983, an article in the IPRA *Newsletter* raised some such research questions and posed the five following hypotheses as possible guidelines for inquiries into the relationship between women and peace. Some of the questions were subsequently been pursued in more recent research.

1. The structural relationships which link economic exploitation in general, oppression of women in particular, the arms trade and military repression are manifestations of the fundamental patriarchal nature of the global dependency-dominance system.
2. Feminism is a significant counterforce to militarism and offers useful approaches to processes for demilitarization.
3. Militarization is a fundamentally misogynist policy resulting from excessive emphasis on masculine modes, values and priorities in the conduct of public affairs.
4. Militarization cannot be adequately analyzed without including an analysis of the social-political aspects of sexism and the common underlying psychological cause of both.
5. Peace research is contaminated by the same sexist bias as affects other social sciences, and, therefore, needs to devise a more balanced perspective on the human condition in order to derive valid data, adequate to provide a knowledge base for the derivation of a global demilitarization process. (Reardon, 1983)

At its biennial meeting in 1986, IPRA finally gave formal recognition to this new area of peace research by establishing a commission devoted to the topic. The present IPRA Study Group on Women and Peace is now a very active and productive section of the association. Thus, the peace research field has begun to acknowledge the links between sexism and militarism and the need for a more balanced perspective. This work has been characterized by the feminine attributes described elsewhere in this book. It is also providing a more gender-balanced perspective on the fundamental issues of equality, development, and peace.   While women have certainly contributed to traditional peace research, their notable contributions, as Boulding points out, are in new conceptual frameworks that put more emphasis on understanding human interaction and social processes than on data gathering. Boulding notes that women researchers were among the first to advocate possibilities for development alternatives not dependent upon the military industrial complex and as Carolyn Stephenson has done to promote inquiry into alternative security systems (Stephenson 1985).

Women researchers also have given considerable attention to the psychological factors that underlie the arms race, how some of these factors relate to masculine identity development, and how deeply embedded they are in our culture and behavior. Some of these factors are revealed in the language of arms development and security analysis, as has been demonstrated by the research of Carol Cohn.

I was curious about the extent to which I might find a sexual subtext in the defense professionals' discourse. I was not prepared for what I found.

I think I had naively imagined that I would need to sneak around and eavesdrop on what men said in unguarded moments, using all my cunning to unearth sexual imagery. I had believed that these men would have cleaned up their acts, or that at least at some point in a long talk about "penetration aids," someone would suddenly look up, slightly embarrassed to be caught in such blatant confirmation of feminist analyses.

... lectures were filled with discussion of vertical erector launchers, thrust-to-weight ratios, soft lay downs, deep penetration, and the comparative advantages of protracted versus spasm attacks—or what one military adviser to the National Security Council has called "releasing 70 to 80 percent of our megatonnage in one orgasmic whump."

But if the imagery is transparent, its significance may be less so. I do *not* want to assert that it somehow reveals what defense intellectuals are really talking about, or their motivations; individual motives cannot necessarily be read directly from imagery, which originates in a broader cultural context. The history of the atomic bomb project itself is rife with overt images of competitive male sexuality, as is the discourse of the early nuclear physicists, strategists, and members of the Strategic Air

Command. Both the military itself and the arms manufacturers
are constantly exploiting the phallic imagery and promise of
sexual domination that their weapons so conveniently suggest.
Consider the following, from the June 1985 issue of *Air Force
Magazine*: Emblazoned in bold letters across the top of a two-
page advertisement for the AV-88 Harrier II—"Speak Softly and
Carry a Big Stick." The copy below boasts "an exceptional thrust-
to-weight ratio," and "vectored thrust capability that makes
the . . . unique rapid response possible."

Much of the sexual imagery I heard was rife with the sort of
ambiguity suggested by "patting the missiles." The imagery can
be construed as a deadly serious display of the connections
between masculine sexuality and the arms race. But at the same
time, it can also be heard as a way of minimizing the seriousness
of militarist endeavors, of denying their deadly consequences. A
former Pentagon target analyst, in telling me why he thought
plans for "limited nuclear war" were ridiculous, said, "Look,
you've gotta understand that it's a pissing contest—you gotta
expect them to use everything they've got." This image says,
most obviously, that this is about competition for manhood, and
thus there is tremendous danger. But at the same time it says
that the whole thing is not very serious—it is just what little boys
or drunk men do.

Another set of images suggests men's desire to appropriate from
women the power of giving life. At Los Alamos, the atomic bomb
was referred to as "Oppenheimer's baby"; at Lawrence Livermore,
the hydrogen bomb was "Teller's baby," although those who
wanted to disparage Teller's contribution claimed he was not the
bomb's father but its mother. In this context, the extraordinary
names given to the bombs that reduced Hiroshima and Nagasaki
to ash and rubble—"Little Boy" and "Fat Man"—may perhaps
become intelligible. These ultimate destroyers were the male
progeny of the atomic scientists. The entire history of the bomb
project, in fact, seems permeated with imagery that confounds
humanity's overwhelming technological power to destroy nature
with the power to create: imagery that converts men's destruction into their rebirth. Laurence wrote of the Trinity test of the
first atomic bomb: "One felt as though he had been privileged to
witness the Birth of the World." In a 1985 interview, General
Bruce K. Holloway, the commander in chief of the Stategic Air
Command from 1968 to 1972, described a nuclear war as involving "a big bang, like the start of the universe."

... I believe that those who seek a more just and peaceful world have a dual task before them—a deconstructive project and a reconstructive project that are intimately linked. Deconstruction requires close attention to, and the dismantling of, technostrategic discourse. The dominant voice of militarized masculinity and decontextualized rationality speaks so loudly in our culture that it will remain difficult for any other voices to be heard until that voice loses some of its power to define what we hear and how we name the world.

The reconstructive task is to create compelling alternative visions of possible futures, to recognize and develop alternative conceptions of rationality, to create rich and imaginative alternative voices—diverse voices whose conversations with each other will invent those futures. (Cohn 1987, 17-24)

Such contributions make it quite clear that, just as women's participation and perspectives are needed in the policy-making process on issues related to peace, they are equally necessary in deriving the knowledge on which the policy is based. As the uses of language alone indicate, women seem to think differently from men.

Women in Peace Education:
Changing the Culture of Violence

With the Declaration on the Preparation of Peoples for Life in Peace (1982), the UN reinforced the need for peace education, advocated virtually for centuries by peace educators and by UNESCO since its founding in 1948. Women's roles, contributions, and leadership in peace education have been many and varied. As parents, women have the opportunity to be the first peace educators of young children since mothers still tend to spend more time with their young children. Serving as the majority of primary school teachers, women also have a profound influence on building the foundations of formal education so that attitudes toward peace and learning about peacemaking are nurtured. In recent years, women have exercised leadership in peace education at the secondary level and in the rapidly expanding field of peace studies in colleges and universities. Over the past three decades, women have, as well, played a very significant part in the conceptual and pedagogic development of peace education. As in other fields related to peace and security, women have been the first to recognize the need for peace education and have facilitated most of what has occurred in its development.

An Australian feminist and peace activist, Nancy Shelley, has offered this brief but broad definition and description of peace education:

> *Peace Education* is concerned with: respect for persons, personal relationships, conflict resolution, social justice, sharing the world's resources, cooperation and community. Peace Education deals with oppression, sexism, racism, injustice and a recognition that violence has to do with power. Peace Education involves a radical approach to curriculum, the structure of schools and the personal relationships within schools. Peace Education is concerned for the planet, the environment and the connectedness of humans to other life. Peace Education will make a study of war and its causes; will consider alternative ways of dealing with conflict, developing the machinery for resolving conflict internationally, nationally, and personally. Peace Education is not confined to schools but involves the community as it moves to affect the whole of society. Once more, I leave you to continue the list. (Shelley 1982)

Peace education, women peace educators argue, is a lifelong process that can take place in every situation in which human beings learn, including the family, the schools and universities, local communities, community organizations, places of worship, workplaces, unions, labor and professional organizations, halls of government and diplomacy, and intergovernmental and nongovernmental organizations. In short, women have demonstrated that peace education can and should be part of every structure and process through which people and societies learn and conduct their public affairs.

From a survey of American curricula for peace education, most of it developed by women, three central concepts have emerged as a core value system that informs peace education (Reardon 1988). Not surprisingly, the three core values concepts echo the same principles that are found in a feminist definition of comprehensive, authentic security and in the themes of the International Women's Decade. The value system of comprehensive peace education comprises: *planetary stewardship*, respecting and preserving the health and integrity of the earth, a notion that complements ecologically sustainable *development*; *global citizenship*, taking responsibility for order and justice in the world community, a process that is a true expression of *peacemaking*; and *positive human relationships*, relating to other persons, nations, and ethnic and ideological groups in a way that acknowledges the human dignity and human rights of all individuals and all societies, principles that are the basis for *equality* between women and men and among the Earth's peoples.

While these concepts are central to peace education in the formal curriculum at all levels, they also inform peace education as it is pursued in nonformal settings. The first, and maybe the most significant, of which may be the family. Parents, and especially mothers, as noted above, are the first peace educators. The mothers of the world, who provide the care for most young children, are fundamental and formative peace educators. Thus, peace education for women should be an important educational priority, and dignity and respect for women in the family is also essential to teaching peace. The very first lesson in one of the three central concepts of peace education, positive human relationships, when it occurs in two-parent families, comes from the relations between the parents. A relationship of equality and mutual respect between them is the foundation of family life for peace.

Parents, partnered and single, especially mothers, have begun to be intentional about "parenting for peace" and instilling a sense of responsibility for creating positive human relationships in the family, the community, and the world. As much as possible, they involve the entire family in peacemaking activities that range from peaceful and amicable resolution of family conflicts to ways of family living that are ecologically responsible and mindful of the needs of the poor. The family is so significant an arena of peace education that the University for Peace, established by the United Nations in Costa Rica in 1980, organized a program on Family Life Education for Peace as a special course in 1987. The most widely known parenting-for-peace book was written by the parents of four children who have made their family life an experience in peace education (McGinnis and McGinnis, 1981). The McGinnis family has made a conscious effort to develop an awareness of injustice that will inspire the children to act to change it. They pay special attention to the inequities between men and women and between rich and poor nations and people.

One of the most important vehicles through which young children learn about war, peace, and conflict inside and outside the family is through their games. Parents, teachers, and religious leaders working together have taken up the struggle against games of competition and toys of violence, both very prominent in the play of youngsters, particularly in industrial, weapons-producing countries.

Competitive games, especially those that can physically endanger the young, have long been a source of anxiety to mothers, especially mothers of sons, whose worries are often ridiculed by fathers who want their sons to be fully prepared for the rough-and-tumble of the competitive masculine world. In recent years, educators and even some athletes have spoken out publicly about the damage youngsters experience in such games, including both physical injuries and emotional harm from either being unable to physically excel or losing in competition. Many schools and playgrounds have begun to introduce cooperative games that are equally or more conducive to the healthy physical development of children and certainly more productive of prosocial attitudes and peaceful behavior. Many mothers and educators believe that competitive team sports still carry the same psychological and social consequences for which they were originally designed. They prepare young men to accept the ultimate competitive game, war, as a socially acceptable practice and an inevitable part of life. Women concerned with peace believe that if war is to become less acceptable and understood as an avoidable consequence of human choice, our young need to be socialized and educated to value cooperation and to seek alternatives to war rather than value competing and winning.

The inevitability and acceptability of war are imprinted on the minds of very young children by the widespread availability of war toys, again mainly in the richer countries and the arms-producing countries. Mothers and educators all over the world have organized against the production and sale of war toys, which have been outlawed in Denmark. Indeed, in that country the law prohibits physical punishment of children, a painful experience many developmental psychologists believe to increase tendencies toward aggressive and violent behaviors. Conferences on war toys, many organized by women, have been held to educate parents and the public about the consequences of such playthings and to emphasize peaceful, creative alternatives to toy guns, bombers, and tanks. Serious study has been conducted about the attitudinal consequences of advertising such toys and their effects on children's play and learning. Women all over the world have organized movements against war toys. Among them are Play for Life in New Zealand, Toys for Peace in the Philippines, and Parents for Peaceful Play in the USA.

The inevitability of war is also the lesson taught by many history texts. Many books contribute to the stereotyping of other cultures and nations and to the reinforcement of enemy images and images of women as less capable than men. If mutual understanding among nations is to be promoted by school curricula, many of the current textbooks must be changed or replaced. Textbook review projects are conducted by several organizations, research institutes, and UNESCO.

Feminist peace educators have been among the pioneers in new forms of learning that emphasize cooperative learning and conflict resolution. Teaching about alternatives to violence and approaches to cooperation has become an important element of peace education in elementary and secondary schools throughout the world. Teachers of young children and adolescents have developed methods and materials for a wide variety of approaches to teaching conflict resolution, peacemaking, and the pursuit of justice. Many have worked cooperatively, nationally and internationally, to exchange ideas and support each other's efforts. Various NGOs are active in the field and offer assistance to those seeking to undertake peace education programs. Among them are the World Confederation of Organizations for the Teaching Profession, the World Council for Curriculum and Instruction, the World Education Fellowship, The School as an Instrument of Peace, Teachers for Peace, and the Peace Education Commission of the International Peace Research Association.

IPRA's Peace Education Commission (PEC) has been a major agency for illuminating the links between women and peace and the interrelationship between these topics and peace education. Making these connections is consistent with PEC's comprehensive approach. The members of this commission have contributed to the most significant theoretical developments in the field of peace education.[5] They have also made clear some of the significant links among development, women, and peace, and the relationship of violence against women to the larger violence of war. As this commission explored the fundamental causes of war and violence, seeking to develop a form of education to reduce and eliminate them, they came to see that these linkages must be integrated into both peace education and peace research. In fact, the Peace Education Commission convened IPRA's 1983 Consultation on Women, Militarism and Disarmament that defined the linkages as a continuum of violence.

UNESCO has also played a very important initiating and catalytic role in peace education. Two of the most significant documents in the field were produced by the organization—the 1974 Recommendation on Education for International Cooperation and Peace and Education regarding Human Rights and Fundamental Freedoms, and the 1980 Final Document of the World Congress on Disarmament Education. Although neither speaks specifically to the significance of the relationship between women and peace, nor reflects a feminist perspective, they offer a comprehensive view of the field compatible with women's perspectives and reflect the important interrelationships among security, disarmament, development, human rights, and peace. Women peace educators played an important role in formulating both documents.

In the past decade, feminist perspectives on peace education have exerted a significant influence on the field. Issues and relationships such as those described in an article by Costa Rican peace educator Celina Garcia in the *Bulletin of Peace Proposals* are now being integrated into peace education.

Whereas for psychology and literary criticism *androgyny* means a union between the masculine and feminine principles, or choosing the best qualities of both sexes, in the peace theory herein discussed, it means the identification and exposure of the modern myths that justify direct violence in the male sex and indirect violence in the social context. This means that if we are seriously considering the possibility of teaching this generation non-violent conflict resolution, the first step should be to find out which mechanisms have placed the burden of violence upon our males and which myths justify this behaviour, as they simultaneously thwart the female initiative. Finally, androgyny means the production of new cultural materials that can eventually substitute our Western culture with a more egalitarian social life no longer based on the cult of violence and oppression.

Peace education seen from this androgynous perspective requires the fusion of Peace Research, Peace Education and Peace Action (PREA), since its principles are: a constant, methodical questioning of social values and social interactions; the development and creation of pedagogical concepts in more harmony with other human beings and nature; research into more peaceful societies where males exist without the use of violence; learning about the non-violent movements, past and present; the active participation in decisions and the careful study of misogyny and the glorification of male violence.

Androgyny may be considered the frame of mind that prepares us for the radical change of being first human and last follower of a sex role that may be in total divergence with temperament or personal desire. Through PREA this change may be translated into concrete messages easily comprehended by the parents and educators concerned about the future of this planet but who have no direct access to international forums or highly academic publications in foreign languages. (Garcia 1981, 163-64)

One major text on the subject, *Education for Peace: A Feminist Perspective* , by Birgit Brock-Utne (1985), has been widely praised. A subsequent edition was published in 1989 (*A Feminist Perspective on Peace and Peace Education*). Brock-Utne argues that we should educate boys in ways more similar to how we educate girls to make them more caring, less competitive, and less war-prone.

The field of peace studies, having gained considerable ground in universities, has also incorporated feminist perspectives and women's issues. A whole section on the theme appears in the university curriculum guide *Peace and World Order Studies* (5th ed.; Klare and Thomas 1988). These developments indicate an acceptance of the argument that without an education sensitive to the socialization patterns that reinforce violence, operating to overcome the disadvantage of the vulnerable, we may not learn to achieve the peace we seek. The type of education urgently needed is one that provides skills in nonviolent conflict resolution and effective modes of cooperation, one that teaches us new ways of thinking, that can produce the kinds of creative approaches we have noted as contributions of women peace researchers and peace activists. As indicated in the quotations from Belenky et al. and Robin Burns in the following chapter, women's ways of knowing offer approaches to new thinking. These new ways are being applied to peace studies by such leaders in the field as Linda Forcey, one of the founders of the Peace Studies Association, among those feminist scholars who continue to keep women's issues on the peace studies agenda while encouraging the field to become more comprehensive and holistic. It is through peace studies that new thinking can be introduced throughout higher education. Feminist academics are sensitive to this opportunity.

Conclusion: Policy Implications

In an attempt to gain a voice in policy making, women are now playing an increasingly significant role in the struggle for peace. Their numbers are woefully few in the councils that make public policy and even fewer in those that make security policy, but they have nonetheless become a voice clearly heard by larger and larger numbers of the public. Women are also becoming more insistent on being heard by the policymakers. Although only four out of the eight hundred world decision makers determining nuclear weapons policy are women (McLean 1986), there are groups such as Women for a Meaningful Summit that are meeting face to face with world leaders (one in Geneva in 1986, in Brussels in 1987, and as Women for Mutual

Security in Baghdad in 1990). They are raising the crucial questions, offering positive policy alternatives, and supporting those few constructive proposals coming from established leadership such as the Five Continents Initiative on nuclear weapons, the Contadora proposals for a peaceful settlement of the Central American crises, the Helsinki 2000 Appeal, the initiatives of President Gorabchev, and the conflict resolution work of President Carter. Women are presenting cogent, general analyses and sound action proposals for change.

> The world is looking to women to bring about change. We expect much from them. The women's councils are like storage batteries of female energy and initiative. Theirs is a mission of paramount importance. Working at grass roots, in every city, every village, factory, neighbourhood, house, a women's council can know better than anybody else the problems of women and their families, help them in good time, in co-operation with local authorities whenever necessary. (Gorbachev 1987)

In *The Nairobi Forward Looking Strategies*, we have a map for the future direction of intentional change, designed to open to women their rightful place in social, economic, and political life and to offer to the world community the benefits of women's participation in the struggle to achieve a full, just, and peaceful world order. Clearly, every effort must now be made to increase women's effectiveness by giving more attention to their voices and ways of thinking and knowing, by lobbying for the implementation of *The Nairobi Forward Looking Strategies* and, in the United States, the ratification of the Convention on All Forms of Discrimination against Women, and most especially by increasing the numbers of women in policy-making positions. This is a process in which all men as well as women, youth, adults, students, workers, professionals, and parliamentarians can participate.

For Reflection and Discussion

1. What are the probable social and psychological factors that deter women's inclusion in equal numbers in national and international political structures? Why is there such emphasis on the paucity of women in high-ranking positions in the United Nations?
2. What is your assessment of Boulding's suggestions for particular ways in which women, under the auspices of the UN and within nongovernmental organizations, might take active parts in peacemaking processes? What other possibilities can you think of?

3. How can we redress the imbalance in the distribution of wealth, power, and time between men and women? What specific steps would be effective in redressing this imbalance in this and other countries? How might a more equitable distribution of social benefits help to change the war system?

4. What feminine values are most sorely needed in the international arena? Can we be assured that the participation of greater numbers of women in international affairs will result in serious consideration of these values? Can you identify male leaders who exemplify and apply these values? While we await these increased numbers of women in diplomacy and foreign affairs, what other measures can be used to introduce these values into policy making?

5. Birgit Brock-Utne has asserted that girls' education tends to be more consistent with the goals of peace education while boys are educated for competition and war. Do you agree? Whatever your position, provide concrete examples to validate it.

For Reading and Further Study

Elise Boulding. 1977. *Women in the twentieth century world.* New York: Sage Publications. The history of women's participation in war and peace activities is discussed, as are women's attempts to increase their political participation. Emphasis on women's participation in NGOs.

Kathy Bickmore. 1987. *A manual for teaching non-violence to youth and adults.* Cleveland: Alternative to Violence Education Project. Provides educational approaches to questions of power and conflict in the context of social issues and global problems.

Jean Bethke-Elshtain. 1981. *Private Man, Public Woman.* Princeton, N.J.: Princeton University Press. An analysis of the political philosophy that underlines the power division and sex-role separation between women and men.

Brigit Brock-Utne. 1989. *Feminist perspectives on peace and peace education.* New York: Pergamon Press. A convincing argument for feminist ideology as the correct and conducive framework from which to educate for, build, and achieve peace in the broadest sense. Part of the Athene series on feminist scholarship.

V. Spike Peterson. 1992. *Gendered states: Feminist revisions of international relations therory.* Boulder: Lynne Reinner. A collection of essays providing feminist alternatives to traditional international relations theory.

Betty Reardon. 1988. *Comprehensive peace education.* New York: Teachers College Press. Arguments and approaches for an integral, holistic approach to peace education.

Nancy Schneidewind. 1987. *Cooperative learning, cooperative lives.* New York: W.C. Brown Publishers. Theoretical bases and practical teaching approaches to cooperative learning as a means to socialize and educate for peace.

J. Ann Tickner. 1992. *Gender in international relations: Feminist perspectives on achieving global security.* New York: Columbia University Press. A feminist critique of the gender bias in international relations theory which endangers global security.

Five

Women's Visions of Peace: Images of Global Security

The need for women's perspectives on human development is critical since it is in the interest of human enrichment and progress to introduce and weave into the social fabric women's concept of equality, their choices between alternative development strategies and their approach to peace, in accordance with their aspirations, interests and talents.

— FLS, para. 6

Toward a Nonviolent World: Women's Ways of Knowing

The importance of introducing women's thinking into public affairs, recognized in *The Nairobi Forward Looking Strategies*, reflects a recent trend in feminist scholarship. Over the past several years, research into women's ways of knowing, reasoning, and decision making has demonstrated that, at least in Western countries,[1] women's thinking is different from that of men; and it has been argued, as noted above, that this difference can shed new light on, and often produce unprecedented solutions to, some of the world's major problems. With regard to issues of security and peace, as has been recounted, women's thinking has already contributed significantly constructive directions. These "feminine" modes of thinking and problem solving can be learned and applied by both women and men; thus, as indicated earlier, they are an important influence in peace education.

Women's thinking and learning develops best when women's identities, values, and perspectives are affirmed in the learning process. They tend to learn most as "connected knowers" whose learning takes place in, and is related to, community. The significance of affirming identities and confirming learners as bearers of knowledge of value to the community has, I would argue, great significance to learning for global community building. Women's ways of knowing may well be applicable to others such as traditional peoples who, like women, have had little voice in global policy making.

> In the masculine myth, confirmation comes not at the beginning of education but at the end. Confirmation as a thinker and membership in a community of thinkers come as the climax of Perry's story of intellectual development in the college years. The student learns, according to Perry, that "we must all stand judgment" and must earn "the privilege of having [our] ideas respected." Having proved beyond reasonable doubt that he has learned to think in complex, contextual ways, the young man is admitted to the fraternity of powerful knowers. Certified as a thinker, he becomes one of Them (now dethroned to lower-case them). This scenario may capture the "natural" course of men's development in traditional, hierarchical institutions, but it does not work for women. For women, confirmation and community are prerequisites, rather than consequences of development . . . .

> . . . It is clear from our data that women's sense of self and voice flourish when they become what we call connected and passionate knowers. We argue that educators can help women develop their minds and authentic voices if they emphasize connection over separation, understanding and acceptance over assessment, collaboration over competition, and discussion over debate, and if they accord respect to and allow time for the knowledge that emerges from first-hand experience. We have learned these things by listening to the woman's voice. (Belenky et al. 1986, 25-26)

The mode of learning outlined above as women's ways of knowing may well be what is needed to engage the disparate and conflictual members of world society in a process of common learning for authentic global security. The adversarial proving of merit Belenky et al. allude to as the masculine confirmation process has been a style of politics as well as academics that has produced the very kind of thinking, described by Stephen Kull (1986) and Carol Cohn (1987), that women peace activists have begun to challenge.

Other feminist research, such as that of Carol Gilligan (1984), has shown that women tend to see reality as a set of interconnected experiences and interrrelationships. They measure the desirability of an action in terms of its human consequences, a characteristic often sorely lacking in policy making. Because of their concern with relationships, women tend toward holistic views of the world that focus on problems in their general context over a longer time period, including past as well as future. For example, women in the peace movement tend not to focus on specific weapons in isolation from the overall arms development dynamic, not to see the arms trade as separate from the general condition of world militarization. They tend instead to see the interrelationships among circumstances and trends. They focus on the links among equality, development, and peace, analyzing strategies toward the achievement of each goal in relation to the other two.

The ways in which holistic thinking and connected knowing have influenced feminist approaches to peace education are clearly captured in an article by Robin Burns, an internationally respected Australian feminist peace educator.

As an educator, I am increasingly concerned about the effects on learners of the ways in which knowledge is 'packaged.' I would go so far as to maintain that there has been an increasing fragmentation of knowledge, which can be seen in such examples as the 'two cultures' of science and the arts/humanities, and in the divisions into 'everyday' and 'specialist' knowledge.

The effects of this fragmentation are a decrease in communication, since a 'knowledge package' includes its own logic and language system which makes dialogue between systems at best ambiguous, and a sense of loss of control or power by individuals who are unable to gain a perspective on the different packages.

In this paper I wish to examine this question of connections and to suggest a perspective which may throw light on ways of thinking about some important world issues and their interconnections. The three issues are development, disarmament and the role of women in society. One major reason for this choice is their bearing on the issue of survival, as a minimum condition, and justice as a central value, which demand that all three issues be faced and acted upon.

Seeing Connections in the Social World

Development and peace are deep human desires which are frustrated by the present distribution of power. Perhaps the most widespread means for maintaining such a situation is the process of socialisation, the ways in which not only detailed

knowledge, skills and values are transmitted from one generation to the next, but also the frameworks for acting in and
reflecting on the world.

The ways in which we learn about the world have important
implications for the images on which we act and think about
ourselves and our relationships with others, our sense of our own
worth and that of others, and how we act—or feel unable to act—
in the world. Many agencies for socialisation, such as schools and
the media, seem dedicated to maintaining the status quo. They
present static images, and ones which are so bounded in time and
space that the possibility for making connections is discouraged
or even excluded . . . .

Inter-relationships: a perspective

Violence, understood in structural terms, links underdevelopment, lack of peace and discrimination based on biological
characteristics. A structurally violent situation is one in which
the means for the satisfaction of basic needs, for the expression
of these and for the attainment of certain rights is controlled by
the group in power, removing not only power but the right to
define oneself from those who are controlled. Thus:

(i) *Development and peace* are reciprocally linked if peace is
defined not as the absence of war but as the achievement of
positive social and cultural goals. The oppressive structures,
which limit or deform development in the interests of the rich
and powerful, trade on insecurity to justify armaments and draw
ordinary people into their folly, partly through denial of alternative ideas and contacts. The violence is also seen in the amount
of money spent on arms, especially when this is compared with
development aid: thus tying resources to destruction and threat
rather than improvement of the human lot. One particular
aspect of this is the development of high technology which is
increasingly associated with the military and the implications of
this as a 'development model,' as well as the tying up of one-third
of the world's scientists in military and para-military research.

(ii) *Development and women.* The development model most
favoured as a universal ideal is the product of men. In practice,
it is men who benefit most from its application. It has now been
established that the mechanisation of agriculture, for example—

considered necessary to increase food production and export crops in particular—is almost exclusively a male preserve. This has two main effects on women, especially when mechanisation is accompanied by the migration of male labour, increases in women's burden through new divisions of labour which leave women behind as the sole food suppliers for the family, and often a reallocation of only the more distant and infertile land for this task. Denied access to education, or given education considered 'appropriate' to some notion (derived in many cases from male anthropologists) of female traditional roles, the sexual divisions of labour and power are widened. And the sorts of cottage industries encouraged to help women earn a cash wage increase their dependence, since the objects made are often for the unreliable tourist trade which is also a contributing factor in the breakdown of culture. (Burns 1982, 66)

The feminine mode of thinking, which emphasizes such linkages as those among disarmament, development, and peace, as Burns does, demonstrates a preference for problem solving comprised of open communication, free access to information, and honest discussion of differences and dialogue among all concerned. Women, whose experience of conflict has been long and varied, particularly as peacemakers in the family, see the best ways to resolve conflicts as those that help to meet at least some of the concerns of all conflicting parties, what has come to be called "win-win solutions." This familial or kinship model of conflict resolution, in which maintaining constructive human relationship is a primary concern, seeks fairness and reconciliation rather than victory and retribution. The ultimate and fundamental human values affirmed by feminism are the sanctity of life and the dignity of persons, so that feminist approaches to conflict resolution place the highest value on the preservation and enhancement of life and maintaining vital, mutually enhancing relationships. Thus nonviolence is a crucial element in feminist peace strategies.

While nonviolence as a philosophy or strategy is not feminist per se, it is consistent with women's modes of thinking and feminist approaches to conflict resolution. Many feminist peace activists are practitioners and advocates of nonviolent change. Women struggling for peace and justice know the world can be very different, and they can and do envision alternative futures in which the peoples of the world can live together so as to enhance the quality of life for all.

Feminine visions of the future involve the achievement of authentic, comprehensive global security. Through such exercises as "imaging a world without weapons," both women and men have envisioned a nonviolent global society. Some have formed networks to refine and work for the achievement of such visions. One example of such a network is the Feminist Utopian Network that grew out of an international conference on Women and the Military System held in Finland in January 1987.

Yet it is not only feminist scholars and peace researchers who have the opportunity to engage in international networks who are working for a nonviolent global society. The movement involves a great variety of women the world over.

From all walks of life, applying feminine values and perspectives to direct non-violent actions for peace have demonstrated ingenuity, creativity, tenacity, and courage. Women have disrupted the patterns of their own lives and risked their careers and well-being in a series of actions throughout the world intended to raise public consciousness about the serious threats to survival and the human costs of the arms race, to demonstrate to their governments their knowledge and concern about these issues, and to bear witness to their personal and corporate commitments to reverse the arms race, to achieve a just international economic order and to ultimately abolish war. As their abolitionist and suffragist grandmothers before them, who helped abolish slavery and enfranchise women, they consistently and insistently declare and work for a more humane and equitable society. And they have achieved much.

Many women in their own homes and communities are making every effort to overcome the violence that pervades society. In their personal relations and families, they practice constructive conflict resolution. They bring up their children in the knowledge that conflict can be conducted constructively, humanely, nonviolently. They encourage cooperation among their children and advocate its emphasis in the schools. They monitor their children's reading, play, and, where TV sets are common in average households, their television viewing—not only to prevent the children's being inundated with messages and images of violence, but also so that they can discuss these images and messages to encourage critical reflection and consideration of alternatives.

In their workplaces outside the home, many women are encouraging more communicative and cooperative, and less competitive, atmospheres. As they demand freedom from sexual harrassment for themselves, they also demand that all workers be treated with dignity. They try to raise issues related to peace, conflict, and disarmament to raise consciousness about the problems and the possibilities for resolution. Many of them who are educators of young children try to convey attitudes of respect for others and knowledge of techniques for nonviolent conflict resolution. Some who are teachers of older children and in universities are active in the development of peace education and peace studies.

In their places of worship and in their community organizations, many women are initiating study-action programs. Many are leaders in peace organizations, and women make up the majority of the volunteer workers who administer and support the programs and demonstrations of the peace organizations that comprise the major part of the worldwide peace movement. They are as well the backbone of the disarmament movement and provide the major source of energy for the NGOs that spearhead that movement and the related campaigns for human rights, development, and the environment.

Women can do and are doing, much to bring about a nonviolent world. But perhaps the most effective thing women can do is to become significant voices in policy making, to bring feminist perspectives, feminine values, and feminine modes of thought into equal consideration with masculine perspectives, values, and modes in confronting the major questions of peace and security. Certainly women should make every effort toward the implementation of the Nairobi Forward Looking Strategies for the Advancement of Women. These measures call for women's input into all aspects of peacemaking, from the highest levels of policy making and international negotiation through the educational process in all spheres and at all levels, including the local, grassroots level where the full impact of war and militarism are felt and where the basic constituency for peace must be built. At all of these levels of policy making and implementation, and in all these spheres of action, there is need of both the energies and the concrete contributions of women, but also, and most especially, of women's views and experience and feminine values and perspectives.

The Nairobi Forward Looking Strategies lay stress on women's participation in decision making in regard to public policy and technology, especially at the regional and international levels, and set a specific goal for the UN "All bodies and organizations of the United Nations system should therefore take all possible measures to achieve the participation of women on equal terms with men at all levels by the year 2000" (FLS, para. 356). Similar goals for all public policy-making bodies are being actively pursued by women throughout the world in their local communities, in provincial and national politics, and in international organizations. Such goals can be enhanced by the implementation of the strategies. The UN secretary general himself has called for more women's participation.

> The world-wide contribution of women to the promotion of peace, to social equity, and to global development is increasingly evident. So, too, is the degree to which women suffer from the persistence of conflict, from hunger and malnutrition, and from an unending arms race. More than ever, women are becoming active in seeking to overcome these negative phenomena. In this they have demonstrated commitment and determination, standing in the forefront in pursuit of the requirements of a peaceful global society. Women have brought energy and inspiration to the struggle for social justice and economic progress to the common benefit of all humanity, regardless of sex, race or belief.

> Unfortunately, women remain inadequately represented at national and international decision-making levels. Where women's views and experience are absent, the political process remains incomplete.

> . . . It must be the mutual goal of governments, intergovernmental and non-governmental organizations, and of individuals to act for the preservation of peace, for sustained economic development and for social justice. The full and equal participation of women in these endeavours is essential. While there is ground for encouragement in the progress achieved during the United Nations Decade for Women, work must continue towards full implementation of the Nairobi Forward Looking Strategies for equality between women and men in all spheres of life. (Perez de Cuellar 1987)

Thus, one of the primary things women can do for a nonviolent world is to work to assure that the implementation of the strategies is monitored and that national policies and programs are derived consistent with the goals and purposes of the International Women's Decade. Continued cooperation between intergovernmental agencies and nongovernmental organizations is essential to this end, as is the continued infusion of feminine thinking and its capacities for imaging peace. Women's ways of knowing, rooted in connectedness, cooperation, and discussion, have enabled women to envision a transformed world characterized by real human security.

Imaging an Alternative Future

Because women carry most of the social responsibilities for nurturing and preparing the young for their adult lives, anticipating the needs of aging relatives, and struggling for community improvements to assure a better quality of life, they are practical futurists. Many have developed the capacity to live in two realities. On the one hand, they have mastered the arts of survival and nurturance within the context of the present reality of conflict, human suffering, and inadequate resources. On the other hand, they also exercise capacities to envision a better world and to struggle for its achievement as they see to the daily needs of those in their care. Women's lives, women's movements, and women's peace organizations are animated by clear and positive visions of a world at peace. While there may be no common definition of peace with which all women throughout the world would agree, this book attempts to demonstrate that there are emerging notions of what constitutes peace and how it can be achieved. Some are even envisioning, in systematic, intentional programs, what peace would be like, how it would affect our daily lives and the social structures in which we live them.[2] Such visions provide images of a transformed world that inform and energize women's efforts for peace. Four such visions reflect the major issues of peace and security, as they are addressed in this book, reviewed in major UN reports,[3] and reflected in UN conventions and standards on human rights. Each vision reflects women's concepts of authentic global security.

The four visions: "The birthright vision" images a world in which the basic human needs of the Earth's people are met; "the vision of women as equal partners" centers on the full equality of women and men in the public and the private spheres; "the transcendence of violence vision" projects a world free of war and the physical abuse of women; and "the vision of an ecological community" perceives a world built on common interests and sharing, and respect and care for planet Earth. All four . are distinct dimensions of the comprehensive image women hold of a total system of authentic global security. Each vision reflects possibilities for meeting a fundamental human need or expectation of well-being, and offers a goal against which to measure progress toward overcoming the various forms of violence and peacelessness described in this book.

The Birthright Vision: Vision of an Equitable World Order

Because women's visions of global security are comprehensive and universal, the alternatives they seek offer authentic security to the whole human family. The first and most fundamental vision is one in which the essential security requisite of the fulfillment of basic human needs would be not only the aspiration of security policy planners but the primary criteria by which policy choices are made. If such were the case, women believe, the minimal security expectations of every child born into the world would assure them fulfillment of these basic needs:

- Food in adequate amounts, and of appropriate types and quality, to assure normal growth and physical development
- A home in a clean, sturdy structure appropriate to the climate and adequate to the size of the family
- Parents or caring guardians whose own basic needs are sufficiently met so that they can in fact fulfill their parenting responsibilities
- A community provided with clean water, basic sanitation facilities, health care services, and education at least at the primary level
- An environment that offers the possibility for sustainable development based on respect for the ecology of the planet, provision of clean air, and preservation of the fundamental natural beauty of the Earth, all essential ingredients in fulfilling the aesthetic needs manifested by all people
- A world community actively committed to the pursuit of peace, justice, and sustainable, ecologically responsible development

Women, particularly mothers and teachers, see such conditions as the basic requirements to be fulfilled for all children if they are to develop, learn, and mature into persons capable of pursuing their unique capacities and becoming responsible, constructive members of society. Indeed, the world community recognized this to be so in 1959 with the Declaration of the Rights of the Child and the Convention on the Rights of the Child adopted by the UN General Assembly in 1989. The convention, in fact, sets forth in detail a set of standards as entitlements of every child, entitlements that provide physical, social, psychological, and cultural security. A world moving toward peace would be a world where the interests of the children and the vulnerable formed major policy criteria. Seeing these possibilities, women's groups such as the Women's International League for Peace and Freedom joined child advocacy groups such as Defense for Children

International to work for the adoption of the convention by the General Assembly, and in a campaign for its ratification by the United States and other nations. All cooperate with UNICEF toward its implementation.

Women as Equal Partners: A Vision of a World of Equality

The nature of women's lives and of the inequalities between men and women is such that throughout most of the world, women, as we have seen, bear a double social and economic burden. Economically, they form a major part of the productive work force in both agriculture and industry, and they produce the entire work force in bearing and raising children. Socially they are responsible for providing the major share of fundamental health care, education, remedial, and compensatory services to those in all kinds of need, usually with resources they must produce themselves. In times of economic stress or social crises, they are called upon to absorb the stresses through the means of household management with little, often no, public assistance. Women provide their societies with fundamental and essential unrecompensed services but have little or no say in deciding the purposes to which these services will be put.

Most of the world's women put in a double work day, rising and retiring hours before and after the rest of the family to perform household chores and provide meals before and after full days in fields, factories, and offices.[4] Women are, and are expected to be, at the service of their families at all hours, under all circumstances. In few societies, and in not too many more individual instances, do men share fully in the tasks and responsibilities of running households and caring for families. Yet they have the almost exclusive right to decide upon the social and economic policies that determine the conditions in which households exist and to dispose of all the resources available to the family. Women, who provide the fundamental bases of the society and the economy, have only a minor share in the benefits of both. Owning less than 1 percent of the world's wealth, they have virtually no power to decide how that wealth will be used, or how the products of their own labors, including their children, will be used by the society, and little or no control over their own time and their own bodies. And, as we have seen, they have been, and are, subject to every possible form of violence, including some particular to their sex.

For centuries many women and men have been aware of these inequities, but comparatively few have sought to remedy them. With the UN's International Women's Decade, however, the attention of the whole world was called undeniably to the injustice of the imbalance in the contributions made by, and the benefits accorded to, women. While the fundamental unjust conditions have not been redressed, the struggle for equity has been universalized and accelerated and is now pursued in light of a vision of equality that would assure an equitable distribution of time, wealth, and power between men and women. Women envision a transformation in the relations between women and men that would bring to the sphere of social and economic management and policy making the perspectives of women and feminine values, on an equal footing with masculine values and perspectives, affording us a more fully human view of social reality and a more holistic approach to public issues, global problems, and world security. Such a transformation would first and foremost renounce violence against wommen and the vulnerable. The vision of human equality arises from the principles articulated by the Universal Declaration of Human Rights and spelled out in the international legal standards created to implement them.

The Women's Decade and the Forward Looking Strategies represent a major challenge to the world community to implement these standards on behalf of women. The Convention on the Elimination of All Forms of Discrimination against Women provides the international legal standards that support and uphold the policy changes called for by the strategies, including a blueprint for change and the concretization of this vision of equality. The survival needs of the human family and their planet home require that the skills, energies, perspectives, and insights of women not be undervalued and repressed by discriminatory laws and customs. Further, if men are to have a greater stake in the continuation of human life and the improvement of its quality, they must take more responsibility for and participate more fully in the activities that provide care and the fulfillment of human needs. A more equal balance between women and men in all spheres of social and family life is essential to the achievement of global security.

So it is that women envision a world in which they share equally with men in guiding and governing the social order and carrying the responsibilities for maintaining and improving the quality of human life. This new vision of the world would be managed by equal numbers of women and men in the policy-making councils, in the legislative halls, in the administrative offices, as well as in all diplomatic delegations and all bodies of the United Nations. In carrying out their responsibilities, these governing and guidance agencies would call equally on the experience and capacities of both women and men. In the formulation of public policy, feminine as well as masculine insights and criteria would be brought to bear. Equal attention would be given to the need for care as to the need to control. Many feminists argue that such equal representation of women and men, of feminine and masculine values, could so change the climate of policy making that the possibilities to transcend war, significantly reduce structural violence, and achieve authentic peace would be greatly enhanced. We could make strides toward a global society in which the rights enumerated in the Universal declaration are actual norms not just aspirations.

The vision of women as equal partners also foresees women playing a significant role in the planning and management of the economy. No longer serving merely as cheap and disposable labor, or as food producers whose production needs are ignored, women would contribute as much with their minds as with their eyes, hands, and backs to the production of economic goods. Such goods when produced by feminine criteria would be more directed to fulfilling human needs, providing authentic economic security rather than the continued technical advancement of war preparations. Public expenditures would be of an entirely different balance between social and military than now reported in *World Military and Social Expenditures*. Serving in such capacities will require equal educational and employment opportunities for women, a condition far different from present circumstances. The 1995 world conference to assess the Forward Looking Strategies should call for more than the 30 percent goal suggested by Boulding and the Economic and Social Council for women's participation in the UN and other policy-making and-implementing bodies. The goal should be expanded to 50 percent.

Such a public world cannot be achieved without comparable changes toward equality in the private sphere, which exerts the main influence over the relations between women and men. If women are to take up equal responsibility for the public order, then they can no longer be expected to carry the major burden of the household and family. In a world of equality, women and men would share these tasks as they would the tasks of running the economy and the polity. Each would contribute equally to the common good of the society and to providing a nurturing environment in the family and the household and strive toward personal relations of equality, complementarity and mutuality. Equality also would pervade educational practice with changes, advocated by feminist peace educators, such as the development of caring and nurturing capacities in boys and men and the enhancement of political and technical capacities in women toward the achievement of a true partnership society (Eisler and Loye 1990).

The vision of women as equal partners is extremely significant in strengthening the possibilities for peace. Enjoying the rich satisfactions of participating in the growth and development of young children enhances the quality of men's lives and provides nurturing male role models as strong as that of the warrior for little boys and adolescent males. Men so invested in the development of the young, in the maintenance of daily life, may well experience greater inhibitions on placing human life at risk through waging or planning wars. They would come in touch with those feminine and nurturant aspects of all human beings that have long inspired the struggle for peace.

Such a world would offer healthier communities and a stronger social order with all members equally considered, concerned, and invested in the success of public policy. This vision is far from the reality in which we now live. However, it is a vision of a practical possibility, a possibility that informs the international human rights standards and inspires women's movements and peace and human rights movements throughout the world.

The Transcendence of Violence: Vision of a Demilitarized and Disarmed World

Women suffer the violence of the world on three levels. As has been described, they are themselves the victims of the generalized violence of war and oppression and of special forms of violence inflicted specifically on women. They suffer the pain of often being helpless to save their loved ones and those in their care from the violence of armed conflict and economic structures that impose cruel deprivations. They are the victims of the violation of the integrity of their persons by sexual abuse and rape, by lack of control over their own bodies. And they suffer, as well, from caring deeply about the plight of all who fall victim to the disasters resulting from militarism and militarization.

Women the world over yearn for a world in which order is maintained by consensus, goals are pursued by constructive rather than destructive means, conflict is resolved without violence, and women are free of the constant fear of sexual harassment and rape. These yearnings lead women to envision a disarmed, demilitarized world in which violence has become a tragic aberration rather than the social norm. The vision of the transcendence of violence brings forth an image of a world constructed on the basis of some of the fundamental values of global feminism. First, the sanctity of the Earth, underlying traditional peoples' reverence for nature, is now essential to preserving our planet. Another value focuses on the oneness of humanity, recognizing the universality of human needs and aspirations, and calls us to understand that the human species will survive or perish together. And last, an emphasis on the integrity of persons demands that the inequities of the global economy and political system be reformed by such measures as a New International Economic Order and a respect for the human rights of all persons. These life-affirming values, when applied to present world conditions, clarify the extent and nature of the violence of the world and the severe and insidious consequences of world militarization.

Militarization, as Ruth Sivard and other peace researchers have demonstrated, has increased apace with the spiraling arms race. With the arms race came an erosion of the fragile trends toward human liberation and the fulfillment of fundamental rights and freedoms that seemed so vigorous at the end of World War II.[5] Indeed, the tragic truth is that within a few short years of the promulgation of the Universal Declaration of Human Rights, the trend toward its realization was reversed, and an alarming increase in its violation has been documented annually by intergovernmental and nongovernmental organizations. During the 1970s and 1980s especially, gross violations were on the increase. Often committed in the name of national security, repression of civil liberties, disappearances, and torture still infected politics and almost invariably accompanied the exertion of the power of the military and the imposition of military rule and militarist values. The militarization of the world also strengthened institutionalized commercial prostitution and other forms of sexual slavery. However, while armed conflict has been on the increase, it has been only one of the direct causes of higher levels of violence against women. Industrialization and corporate enterprises have also spawned new forms of exploitation and prostitution, and although the number of military governments has been reduced in recent years, the legacy of repression and human rights violations continues to be a source of much human suffering. Women, therefore, see the need to devise policies and strategies to reverse all trends toward militarization and to root out the militarist thinking and value system that is the cause of most of the violence pervading our contemporary human experience.

Such policies might be derived from images of a demilitarized world that portray new social institutions, and processes incorporating the values and techniques of nonviolence. Women envision a world in which negotiation, arbitration, mediation, and the rule of law have replaced the role of force and armed conflict to resolve disputes and impose the resolution on the losing party. They envision vast numbers of persons trained in nonviolent conflict management operating at every level of social organization, from the rural village or urban neighborhood to the international level, using skills and techniques now available to all and applying feminist modes of compromise and reconciliation, as a means of achievinng win-win solutions where no one need be a loser.

Women envision a process of transarmament and demilitarization in which national armed forces are gradually replaced by nonviolent civilian defense forces trained in passive resistance and nonthreatening defense postures. They see this reduction of national armed forces as occurring simultaneously with the building of mediation forces and a United Nations standing peacekeeping force that relieves nations of the burden of each being the sole defender of its own interests and borders. They understand that the establishment of such a force would signify the existence of sufficient communal interest to substitute peacekeeping policing mechanisms in the place of preparation for war. The world would have acknowledged that order and cooperation are more in the interest of every nation than the anarchy of an unpredictable and dangerous system of "self-defense." Moving toward a system of "common security" is seen as a way of increasing authentic world security.[6]

Women see the nurturing of international understanding and the building of consensus as developing through cooperative efforts at the resolution of world problems, through more open and regular communication among potential adversaries, through mutual trust building and independent and collaborative initiatives in the reduction of armed forces and the ending of the arms trade. They see the possibilities of major cultural exchanges involving local communities as well as national agencies. They see the savings of resources and reduction of tensions to be gained through economic cooperation and economic conversion.

A demilitarized world would be one in which sexual slavery and sexist repression would be guarded against by world agencies and institutions established to protect and enhance human rights and fundamental freedoms. Rape, enforced prostitution, involuntary pregnancy and the gross exploitation of women's bodies would not be tolerated in a world committed to the development of nonviolent institutions and systems.

What is most essential in this process of transcending violence is the demilitarization of the mind. As we have been instructed by the UNESCO charter, and reminded here in the quotations from Nancy Shelley, Charlene Spretnak, and Carol Cohn, "Wars begin in the minds of men," especially in the minds of men who believe force and violence to be the necessary or appropriate means of achieving human purposes. The willingness to use violence for public purposes stems from a form of thinking that sanctions violence and sees human beings as inherently unequal. As I have argued elsewhere (Reardon 1985), the inequality between women and men has been a fundamental cause of the social toleration of many forms of violence against women, and of the perpetuation of war.

Many women believe that only through a carefully orchestrated, sincerely and zealously pursued process of demilitarization can the violence of the world be reduced—all violence, the direct violence of armed conflict arising from political and ideological struggles and the indirect structural violence of economic exploitation from greed and competition. Understanding the links between military violence and particular forms of violence against women, highlighted by the statement of the IPRA Consultation on Women, Militarism, and Disarmament, previously cited, leads many to see disarmament and demilitarization as important as the reduction of the abuse of women through laws regarding rape, family violence, and economic equity. Both routes must be pursued, but the primary path to the envisioned transcendence of violence is through comprehensive demilitarization of economic and political structures, social custom, and ways of thinking.

Those now working for a demilitarized world are formulating and lobbying for nonmilitary solutions to contemporary international crises, as they strive to educate policymakers about the possibilities for alternative security systems. They have gone directly to the leadership of hostile nations. As did their foremothers before World War I, Women for Mutual Security (see appendix 4 for address) sent a delegation of women to Baghdad in an attempt to avoid the Gulf War. One day before the hostilities were initiated by the United States, they issued the following message to President Bush.

We are a delegation of women representing women's organizations from all over the world, and have just returned from a trip to Baghdad. We spent four days there and had full and lengthy discussions with the following people:

(1)   Mr. Latif Nusaif Jasim, Minister of Culture and Information
(2)   Mr. Saadi Mahdi Salif, President of the National Council
(3)   Mr. Taha Yasim Ramadan, First Deputy to the Prime Minister
(4)   Glanes Aziz, Vice President of the National Council

(5)   Adel Abdel Karim, Foreign Affairs Head, National Council
(6)   The Executive Board of the Federation of Iraqi Women

In all of our discussions with ministers and other officials there was, of course, a common line on the situation and a genuine conviction that Iraq was right in its analysis and evaluation and right in its stand.

Reading between the lines, however, but sometimes from comments made more overtly, we understood that there was flexibility, and a willingness to consider other options along the lines of their proposed peace plan of August 12, 1990. There were no changes in substance, but changes in the tone of the presentation. Clearly they want to sit down and truly discuss the issues.

In more specific terms, we believe the withdrawal from Kuwait is negotiable:

This is why we ask you, have all efforts at peace been made? We believe they have not. Although there have been some sketchy overtures on both sides, the possibilities were allowed to disappear in the shifting sand. One "last effort" is not enough. The last efforts must continue. It is never too late to stop a war.

Our women's plea, and in the name of justice, and for the sake of humanity, we ask you to reject the rivers of blood that will flow in the Gulf region and find a political solution. This is the only solution in harmony with human intelligence and civilized behavior.

Margarita Papandreou, Co-ordinator, Women for Mutual Security
Nawal El Saadawi, Arab Women's Solidarity Federation (Egypt)
Flora Abdrakhmanova, Women's Int'l League for Peace and Freedom, Soviet Women's Committee
Joan Drake, Institute of Policy Studies, Madres (Lat. America), WILPF
Maude Barlow, Voice of Women, Canada, Women World Parliamentarians for Peace
Kay Camp, Women's Int'l League for Peace and Freedom
Fathieh Saudi, Arab Women's Solidarity Association (Jordan)

On behalf of the International Women's Gulf Peace Initiative. (Women for Mutual Security 1991b)

Earlier, on 10 January, 1991, they had explained the nature of their concerns in a statement at a press conference in Baghdad.

We are a delegation of women here in Baghdad representing women'sorganizations from all over the world which came to get a more comprehensive view of the situation, and to see if there was any way we could play a role in an authentic peace process.

As women, there are many elements in this brinksmanship strategy that create deep anxieties for us . . . .

. . . we have the problem of the double standards in international law. We have fought the double-standard in male-female relationships for decades now, so we are particularly sensitive to the hypocrisy of such standards . . . .

And last, but not least, we are against the use of force in settling conflict situations. When people develop the attitude that differences can be settled through violent means, then we perpetuate a mentality that brings violence into all human relations, and right into the home, where women and children are the primary victims. War cannot be diplomacy by other means. War must become obsolete . . . .

Women have always been the true advocates of peace. We believe in living for a cause, not dying for it. If we had the power in our hands, we would sit at the negotiating table, and we would search for as long as it takes for a peaceful solution. Disputes cannot be settled without discussion. (Women for Mutual Security 1991a)

In calling for discussion, these women were calling for not only an alternative approach to conflict, but an alternate way of thinking. The same mode of thinking that sees people as inherently unequal also makes possible the use of violence against others who are perceived as less important, evil, or in opposition to authority. Violence against women, cultural and political repression, as well as war all begin in the minds of men, and all are interrelated. The way we think, and the way we teach the young to think, about the world and others will be the main determinant of the future security of the world. The processes of demilitarization and moral inclusion required to lead us to human equality, a just peace, and authentic global security must begin with the demilitarization of the mind, and that step can be initiated by first becoming fully aware of the nature and extent of violence against women as the main indicator of the general level of violence in the society. Awareness of a problem is the beginning of learning that can change the way we think about the world. Feminist peace researchers argue that there is a need to change our way of thinking so as to see all people as persons equally endowed with dignity, fundamental human rights, and integrity, within one moral community, the universal human community (Opotow 1990). Moral inclusion will lead us to reject the belief in the inferiority of women and the concept that adversaries are not entitled to their human rights; indeed, to transcend the very concept of "enemy" that is fundamental to the war system (Reardon 1985).

An Ecological Community: Vision of Comprehensive Authentic Global Security

When the various visions of global security women have projected merge into one comprehensive vision of global security, we see a world in which all the feminist criteria for security are used to establish social goals and guide policy formation. Such a world would be striving for ecological balance and the health of the biosphere through the application of a comprehensive, exigently observed set of planetary environmental standards. All peoples of the Earth would be adherents to the Earth Covenant, a document drafted by an international group of men and women under the initiative of the feminist peace researcher, cofounder of Global Education Associates, Patricia Mische. The document reflects the belief in the efficacy of observing agreements and standards such as those set forth by the United Nations. Its substance also embodies ecofeminist principles of the organic interrelatedness of living systems and the imperative to survival of nurturing relationships.

We and all living beings depend upon the Earth and upon one another for our common existence, well-being, and development. Our common future depends upon a reexamination of our most basic assumptions about humankind's relationship to the Earth. We must develop common principles and systems to shape this future in harmony with the Earth.

Principles and Commitments

In covenant with each other and on behalf of the whole Earth community, we commit ourselves to the following principles and actions:

- Relationship with the Earth: All Life forms are sacred. Each human being is a unique and integral part of the Earth's community of life and has a special responsibility to care for life in all its diverse forms.

Therefore, we will act and live in a way that preserves the natural life processes of the Earth and respects all species and their habitats. We will work to prevent ecological degradation.

- Relationship with Each Other: Each human being has the right to a healthful environment and to access to the fruits of the Earth. Each also has a continual duty to work for the realization of these rights for present and future generations.

Therefore—concerned that every person have food, shelter, pure air, potable water, education, employment, and all that is necessary to enjoy the full measure of human rights—we will work for more equitable access to the Earth's resources.

- Relationship Between Economic and Ecological Security: Since human life is rooted in the natural processes of the Earth, econnomic development, to be sustainable, must preserve the life-support systems of the Earth.

Therefore, we will use environmentally protective technologies and promote their availability to people in all parts of the Earth. When doubtful about the consequences of economic goals and technologies on the environment, we will allow an extra margin of protection for nature.

- Governance and Ecological Security: The protection and enhancement of life on Earth demand adequate legislative, administrative and judicial systems at appropriate local, national, regional, and international levels. In order to be effective, these systems must be empowering, participatory, and based on openness of information.

Therefore, we will work for the enactment of laws that protect the environment and promote their observance through educational, political and legal action. We shall advance policies of prevention rather than only reacting to ecological harm.

Declaring our partnership with one another and with our Earth, we give our word of honor to be faithful to the above commitments. (Mische 1987, 33)

Standards of well-being much like those listed in the International Covenant on Economic, Social, and Cultural Rights (1966) would be used to steer the human family toward policies designed to meet human needs, in a framework respectful of the limits of the Earth. The statistics that now appear annually in *World Military and Social Expenditures* would be drastically altered as all societies put a higher priority on serving the social needs of their people than on keeping up with a costly and destructive arms race. Relations among nations would be strengthened by a variety of cooperative and confidence-building programs, and peace and security would be maintained by the nonviolent institutions of an alternative security system.

Central to this vision is the process of economic conversion, with a shift in resources from military to civilian production along with a concomitant process of disarmament and the building of peacekeeping capacities so that the world could ultimately achieve general and complete disarmament. The twin tasks of economic conversion for development and disarmament as a process of peacemaking are the main foundations for a planetary human community. Development pursued with a respect for the health of the planet would demonstrate the ecofeminist perspective in global economic policy.

When women's visions take the form of intentional imaging, actual steps, events, and policies are articulated that could bring the vision into being. These histories of the future are sometimes called "transition scenarios." Here is one such feminist transition scenario on how peace might come to the world, devised on the eve of the second special session on disarmament of the General Assembly. It follows actual history until 1992 and then imagines possibilities for the next century. Some details have been added since the first writing.

Disarmament is the major transformational task for our historical period and the key to this transition scenario, which envisions general and complete disarmament as only a first step toward exorcising coercive force from the world political system. When we consider a total peace system as the overall goal, disarmament does not seem so remote or unattainable. It is but one part of the total system. If, as in Elise Boulding's frame of reference, we see an historical period as 200 years, we can look forward and backward at the peace-building process at work and perceive disarmament not as an end but as the turning point. Elise uses the 200-year period primarily to stretch the visioning process in somewhat the same way the World Order people talk about relevant utopias. It places the immediate present's problems in a different dimension and makes them less overwhelming . . . .

I find it helpful to think of disarmament as a turning point in the transition scenario. Disarmament would be the structural manifestation of a commitment to peace, to the reduction of violence and coercive force. If we look at the historical process in a 200-year framework with our era as a turning point, it might look something like the following in terms of historical landmarks:

1899:   The International Court of Justice at the Hague—an attempted institutional alternative to war through the adjudication of international disputes;

1915-17:   Founding of major international women's peace movement—forerunner of Women's International League for Peace and Freedom

1928:   The Kellogg-Briand Pact—a treaty to which more than 50 nations ultimately adhered that renounced war as an instrument of national policy;

1945:   The United Nations Charter that declared its purpose as ending war;

1962:   McCloy-Zorin Agreement on General and Complete Disarmament stating that total disarmament was the ultimate goal of the negotiating process.

1975:   Mexico City Internatioanl Women's Year Conference beginning of UN Decade for Women

1978:   The UN Special Session on Disarmament (SSD I), which declared disarmament as a basic requirement for peace and development; provided an outline of needed steps toward disarmament.

1979:   Convention on the Elimination of All Forms of Discrimination Against Women: more women come into politics.

1980:   Copenhagen mid women's decade conference asserts essential link between women's emancipation and peace.

1982:   The Second Special Session on Disarmament (SSD II) launched the World Disarmament Campaign to inform and educate about the needs and possibilities for disarmament.

1985: • Nairobi Conference formulates Forward Looking Strategies for the Advancement of Women; links women's rights and peace

• Beginning of changes in world political and power relationships.

1991: General Assembly establishes registry to record and control arms trade.

1992: UN Summit on Environment and Development adopts principles for ecologically sound development based on criteria for healthy societies and a healthy planet; Secretary General issues Agenda for Peace; Chemical Weapons prohibition adopted.

1995: International prohibition of the use, production, deployment or development of weapons of mass destruction called for by World Women's Conference, Beijing.

2000: International prohibition of the arms trade results from NGO efforts.

2020: General and Complete Disarmament Agreement (GCDA)—member nations of the UN acknowledge their adherence to a worldwide agreement; total disarmament process begun. Agreement negotiated by an assembly of equal numbers of women and men.

2050: Nonviolence Accord (NVA)—the nations of the world renounce the use of violence as a means to social, economic, and political ends by signing the NVA. Delegates cite the Seville Statement.

2100: Confederation of Human Communities on Planet Earth—formal acknowledgement of an institutionalized system of global peace, based on the Universal Declaration of Human Rights and the Earth Covenant.

In working toward a peace system, by about 2050 we should achieve a Nonviolence Accord. Institutionally and technologically, the accord (NVA) would be preceded by three-quarters of a century of a nation-state system that attempted arms control while continuing to build stockpiles and distribute arms. Those states chose military values and security at the cost of human values and human security. Finally, the deterioration of the quality and potential for continuation of human life becomes so apparent that a major value shift occurs, away from militarism and toward humanism. This shift was largely the result of the women's peace movement struggling to replace military values with human values.

Movement toward NVA begins in the last quarter of the 20th century with various nonviolent strategies applied to actual conflicts, staged disarmament and global institution building that would bring about general and complete disarmament under global institutional control, with compulsory, peaceful conflict-resolution machinery for the settlement of international disputes. A global security force would maintain world security and gradually obtain the exclusive right to use force internationally. National forces trained in nonviolent intervention methods would be reduced to the minimum necessary to preserve domestic order . . . .

The disarmament movement merging with environmental and human rights and women's movements outlines economic and political conversion based on principles of ecological balance and social justice.

By the end of the 21st century the nonviolent social order could be institutionalized into a functioning peace system. The system would be officially inaugurated with a charter for the Confederation of Human Communities on Planet Earth. Such a charter would officially recognize as global regulatory agencies those institutions that the global community had devised over the last century and a half to assure equitable enjoyment of peace and justice by all the peoples of the world, and the health and viability of the planet.

Through the humane application of technology, as envisioned by Boulding and such feminist science fiction authors as Ursula LeGuin, the forces of community and consensus could build so that coercion of any kind, even nonviolent, would simply fade away from the repertoire of socially acceptable human behavior. The former consequence—mutual empowerment of formerly competitive human groups and nation states, even women and men—would enhance the development of the synergic types of power that futurists and feminists envision now. Thus the human capacity to achieve goals would be increased enormously, even to the point of creating such a true peace system by the beginning of the 22nd century. (Adapted and expanded from Reardon 1980)

To envision such possibilities is the first step in bringing them about. Without such visions we cannot move into an uncertain and unknown future, a future that conforms more explicitly to our feminist values. It is from these values of care, inclusion, fairness, nonviolence, mutuality that we determine policies and implementation plans. And it is from today's policies that tomorrow will be born.

Feminist Questions for Assessing Security Policy

I have tried to make two things sharply evident in this review of the relationship between women and peace: the need to change the modes of thinking we bring to issues of national and world security and the need to change the structures that exclude women's full and vitally needed contribution to the peacemaking process. To bring about structural change we need policy change. In other words, just as women are now asserting a new and unprecedented effort to gain a voice and articulate their perspectives to the public, they must also find ways to be heard by policy makers. Feminists in seeking ways to bring women's experience into politics are raising new policy questions based on criteria derived from women's ways of thinking. From such questions, steps toward the evolution of a transition scenario may arise.

As I have tried to demonstrate, women's ways of thinking lead to a distinctly feminine approach to security issues that is quite different from the current approaches to national security applied by the dominantly male political leadership. Throughout, I have tried to demonstrate the need to bring the feminine approach into policy making, and to bring more women into the policy-making process, to introduce feminine perspectives and criteria, and to provide the benefits of women's ways of thinking. The feminine approach suggested here produces a particular set of criteria that women bring to the assessment of security policy. These criteria, like women's visions of a world at peace, derive directly from the four essential security expectations outlined in the introduction that comprise the feminist concept of authentic global security. They can be designated as sustainability, vulnerability, equity, and protection.

Sustainability. Subtainability derives from the expectation that the Earth will sustain life and demands that unnecessary damage to the environment and the natural order and basic resources be avoided. Sustainability is a criterion that requires raising questions about the ecological dimensions and consequences of every policy decision. Any action taken for public purposes may have ecological consequences. Much media attention has been given to personal action and behaviors in regard to "cleaning up" the environment. Equal attention needs to be given to public policy in regard to sustaining and restoring it. Questions about long-term as well as short-run effects on the environment need to be raised in consideration of every public issue. Local as well as potential global impacts must be anticipated. The fundamental question to be asked is whether the policy in question will harm or enhance any of the fragile ecological systems of the Earth. The principles of the Earth Covenant should be applied to every policy in the exercise of the criteria of sustainability. If the Earth is to sustain humanity, then humanity must sustain the Earth.

Vulnerability. Vulnerability derives from the expectation of the meeting of basic human needs and requires that policies not result in further deprivation of the weak and the poor. Vulnerability recognizes the fragility of most life forms, of social systems as well as ecosystems. It recognizes, too, that harm to one part of any system affects the whole system. Deprivation in one sector of society ultimately weakens the whole of society. The structural violence of ignoring the human-needs implications of any policy decision makes the nations and communities experiencing poverty less secure and ultimately the world less secure. Respecting and accounting for vulnerability determine the level of justice in a society. If justice is to be achieved, every policy should be examined in the light of its actual or potential effect on the vulnerable. As every public policy is considered, questions should be raised as to how it will affect the poor and the environment, and whether it will increase or decrease the total deprivation suffered by the human family and the environmental health of the planet. The Convention on the Rights of the Child, the Forward Looking Strategies, the Convention on All Forms of Discrimination against Women and "Agenda 21" issued by the "Rio Earth Summit" on environment and development provide particular indicators for assessing social and ecological vulnerability.

Equity. Equity derives from the expectation that humans will be nurtured by their own societies and necessitates a process of policy making that is based upon full and fair representation of all, and thus requires that the policy-making process involve equal numbers of women and men. Equity ultimately rests on the full and universal recognition of human rights and dignity. Equity in such universal terms can best be assessed by taking account of the effects a policy will have on the human rights of women. Limits on, or denial of, the rights of women affect the rights of others, those who depend on them, the communities in which they live. A policy should be assessed in light of whether it will protect or violate the fundamental rights of any and all groups affected, and the rights of women are the best indicator of the wider effects. In every decision-making process, we should ask what results might accrue to ethnic minorities, indigenous peoples, oppressed persons, as well as women. The Universal Declaration of Human Rights and the conventions derived from it, particularly those related to discrimination against women, racism, and apartheid, provide readily applicable standards of equity.

Protection. Protection derives from the expectation of defense against harm, be it from other persons or groups or from natural and sometimes unexpected sources. It calls for serious efforts both at creating positive, constructive relationships with others and at avoiding putting society at risk of harm of any type—two skills women have perfected over the centuries. It requires more efforts at establishing positive interdependence, and the avoidance of national policies that weaken or damage relationships, create hostilities, or threaten the health and well-being of any sectors of society. It demands the end to the development of ever more "sophisticated" arms and a cessation of the arms trade as the greatest security risks we face. New and creative efforts in international cooperation, confidence building, and conflict resolution must be devised and pursued. Protection from harm, the criterion now most influential in security policy, can best be assured by prevention and anticipation, or avoidance. Protection of peace and security lies in causing no threat to others, preventing harm by not courting it, and certainly not by preparing to harm others, the purpose of arms development. Nonthreatening security systems and measures must be designed and pursued. Communication and negotiation, constant monitoring of issues of controversy and conflict need to become a normal part of all social systems. For every policy, we must ask: Will it threaten or cause harm to others? Will it strengthen or weaken positive, constructive relationships? Will it detract or add to the total security of all? The Final Document of the first special session on disarmament (*Final Document* 1978) provides an excellent set of guidelines for protection through demilitarization and disarmament.

It contains many possibilities to consider in the search for alternative security systems.

In every case, a primary barometer of positive or negative security policy is measured by the effects on women. In light of their visions of security, women are the ones who are, and have been, raising these questions in the interest of all. If women's questions, women's visions, and women's voices can be brought fully into the planning of our future, the problems of peace will be approached from perspectives that will open new and hopeful posssibilities. Feminist visions of global security are inspired by hope and informed by possibilities. Women dream of peace and craft the future from their dreams.

> Let me explain. The dream, the utopia, is a world without weapons. This must be the highest peak a civilization can reach. When our quarrels, our conflicts—which will always exist as long as we are varied and different human beings—are resolved without resort to violence. Our policy will be to prevent the use of arms until they can be eliminated. When we see life between human beings as a partnership and life among nations as a larger partnership, we have the possibility of redirecting this world away from war and violence to one of peace. (Papandreou 1990)

For Reflection and Discussion

1. What values should inform security proposals? What values would inform your vision of global security? Which, if any, of those values would you define as feminist?

2. What conditions would characterize your vision of global security? What obstacles would need to be overcome, what problems resolved, to achieve your vision?

3. What problem-solving strategies might be employed to resolve the problems your vision seeks to eliminate? What events might comprise a transition scenario from now until the achievement of your vision? What indicators would assess progress toward your vision? What groups and movements would need to be enlisted to achieve your vision?

4. What steps can/will you personally take to move the world toward a comprehensive authentic security system?

For Further Reading and Study

Sisella Bok. 1989. *A strategy for peace: Human values and the threat of war*. New York: Pantheon Books. While not specifically feminist in perspective, the author brings a very human voice to practical proposals for achieving peace. Her suggestions are embedded in her vision of change through practical possibilities.

Irene Diamond. 1990. *Reweaving the world: The emergence of ecofeminism*. San Francisco: Sierra Club Press Books. A collection of works that demonstrate the organic, holistic way of thinking ecofeminists are bringing to the resolution of global problems and the envisioning global futures.

Elisabet Sahtouris. 1989. GAIA: *The human journey from chaos to cosmos*. New York: Pocket Books. A reflection on how the evolution of the living Earth can instruct the human family in the development of the "benign technologies" that would characterize some of the feminist visions of peace described here.

Appendix 1

The Universal Declaration of Human Rights
(Excerpts)

Preamble

Whereas recognition of the inherent dignity and of the equal and inalienable rights of all members of the human family is the foundation of freedom, justice and peace in the world . . . .

. . . it is essential . . . that human rights should be protected by the rule of law. . . .

The United Nations . . . Charter reaffirmed . . . faith in fundamental human rights in the dignity and worth of the human person and in the equal rights of men and women. . . .

The General Assembly

Proclaims

THIS UNIVERSAL DECLARATION OF HUMAN RIGHTS as a common standard of achievement for all peoples and all nations, to the end that every individual and every organ of society. . . shall strive. . . to promote respect for these rights and freedoms. . . to secure their universal and effective recognition and observance. . .

Article 1: All human beings are born free and equal in dignity and rights. They are endowed with reason and conscience. . . .

Article 2: Everyone is entitled to all the rights and freedoms set forth in this Declaration, without distinction of any kind, such as race, color, sex. . . .

Article 3: Everyone has the right to life, liberty and security of person.

Article 4: No one shall be held in slavery or servitude; . . .

Article 5: No one shall be subjected to torture. . . cruel, inhuman or degrading treatment or punishment.

Article 6: Everyone has the right to recognition everywhere as a person before the law.

Article 7: All are equal before the law and . . . entitled to equal protection of the law. . . .

Article 8: Everyone has the right to an effective remedy by the competent national tribunals for acts violating . . . rights granted him[1] by . . . law.

Article 9: No one shall be subjected to arbitrary arrest, detention or exile.

Article 10: Everyone is entitled in full equality . . . fair and public hearing by . . . impartial tribunal in the determination of his rights and obligations and of any criminal charge. . . .

Article 11: (1) Everyone charged with a penal offence has the right to be presumed innocent until proved guilty according to law in a public trial. . . .

(2) No one shall be held guilty of any penal offence . . . which -did not constitute a penal offence, at the time committed. Nor shall heavier penalty be imposed than was [previously] applicable.

Article 12: No one shall be subjected to arbitrary interference with his privacy . . . nor attacks upon his honor. . . .

Article 13: (1) Everyone has the right to freedom of movement and residence within the borders of each state.

(2) . . . right to leave any country, . . . and to return to his country.

Article 14: (1) . . . right to . . . asylum from persecution.

(2) [but] not in the case of prosecutions genuinely arising from non-political crimes. . . .

Article 15: (1) . . . right to a nationality.

(2) No one shall be arbitrarily deprived of his nationality nor denied the right to change his nationality.

---

[1] While "everyone" as employed in the Declaration refers to both men and women, as specified in the Preamble only the masculine pronoun is used throughout.

Article 16: (1) Men and women of full age . . . have the right to marry and to found a family. . . .

(2) Marriage . . . only with the free and full consent of the . . . spouses.

(3) The family . . . is entitled to protection by society and the State.

Article 17: (1) Everyone has the right to own property.

(2) No one shall be arbitrarily deprived of his property.

Article 18: freedom of thought, conscience and religion.

Article 19: freedom of opinion and expression . . . information.

Article 20: (1) . . . peaceful assembly and association.

(2) No one may be compelled to belong to an association.

Article 21: (1) . . . right to take part in the government.

(2) . . . equal access to public service

(3) The will of the people [is] the basis of government . . . universal and equal suffrage by secret vote.

Article 22: . . . . social security . . . economic, social and cultural rights indispensable for . . . dignity and the free development of . . . personality.

Article 23: (1) . . . right to work, to free choice of employment, to just . . . conditions of work . . . to protection against unemployment.

(2) . . . equal pay for equal work.

(3) . . . just and favorable remuneration ensuring . . . existence worthy of human dignity, and supplemented, if necessary, by . . . social protection.

(4) . . . right to form and to join trade unions.

Article 24: . . . . rest and leisure, including reasonable limitation of working hours . . . holidays with pay.

Article 25: . . . . standard of living adequate for . . . health and well-being . . . food, clothing housing and medical care . . . security in the event of unemployment, sickness, disability, widowhood, old age. . . .

(2) Motherhood and childhood are entitled to special care .... All children ... shall enjoy the same social protection.

Article 26: (1) ... right to education. Education shall be free, at least in the elementary and fundamental stages ....

(2) Education is for the full development of the human personality ... strengthening of respect for human rights.

(3) Parents choose ... the kind of education given to their children.

Article 27. (1) ... right to participate in the cultural life. ...

(2) ... protection of ... interests resulting from ... scientific, literary or artistic production.

Article 28: ... a social and international order in which the rights and freedoms set forth in this Declaration can be fully realized.

Article 29: Everyone has duties to the community ...

(2) ... only ... limitations [on rights and freedoms] determined by law solely for the purpose of securing due recognition and respect for the rights and freedoms of others.

(3) ... rights and freedoms may in no case be exercised contrary to the purposes and principles of the united Nations.

Article 30: (no) right to engage in any activity ... aimed at the destruction of any of the rights and freedoms set forth herein.

Appendix 2

The Convention on the Elimination of All Forms of Discrimination against Women (Excerpts)*

The Convention on the Elimination of All Forms of Discrimination against Women is essentially an international bill of rights of women and a framework for women's participation in the development process. The most concise and usable document adopted during the UN Decade for Women, it is the result of several decades of work by the UN Commission on the Status of Women and international women's organizations. The Convention spells out internationally accepted principles and standards for achieving equality between women and men. . . .

The thirty articles of the Convention are condensed below. The full text of Convention in any of the UN languages can be obtained from the United Nations Department of Public information in New York or from the Branch for the Advancement of Women in Vienna. Additional materials on the Convention and on CEDAW, Committee on the Elemination of Discrimination Against Women, can be obtained from IWRAW. . .[1]

The International Women's Rights Convention

Countries that have ratified the Convention "condemn discrimination against women in all its forms" and "agree to pursue by all appropriate means and without delay a policy of eliminating discrimination against women" (Article 2). The first five articles of the Convention outline the general premises of eliminating discrimination and the general obligations undertaken by States parties; the last thirteen articles detail the establishment, functioning and administration of CEDAW.

---

*Excerpted for distribution by the International Women's Rights Action Watch (IWRAW). See appendix 4 for address.

Article 1: Definition of Discrimination

> —any distinction, exclusion or restriction made on the basis of sex, which has the purpose or effect of denying equal exercise of human rights and fundamental freedoms in all fields of human endeavor.

Article 2: Policy Measures to be Undertaken to Eliminate Discrimination

> —embody the principle of equality in national constitutions, codes or other laws, and ensure their practical realization
> —establish institutions to protect against discrimination -ensure that public authorities and institutions refrain from discrimination
> —abolish all existing laws, customs and regulations that discriminate against women

Article 3: Guarantees Basic Human Rights and Fundamental Freedoms on an Equal Basis with Men

Article 4: Temporary Special Measures to Achieve Equality

> —temporary special measures may be adopted and must be discontinued when equality is achieved
> —special measures to protect maternity are not considered discriminatory
> —practices based on the inferiority or superiority of either sex shall be eliminated
> —ensure that family education teaches that both men and women share a common role in raising children

Article 5: Sex Roles and Stereotyping

> —social and cultural patterns must be modified to eliminate sex-role stereotypes and notions of the inferiority or superiority of either sex
> —family education shall teach that men and women share a common responsibility in the raising of children

Article 6: Prostitution

> —measures shall be taken to suppress all forms or traffic in women and exploitation of prostitution

Article 7: Political and Public Life

>—the right to vote in all elections and be eligible for election to all elected bodies
>—to participate in formulation of government policy and hold office at all levels of government
>—to participate in non-governmental organizations

Article 8: Participation at the International Level

>—the opportunity to represent their country at the international level and to participate in international organizations

Article 9: Nationality

>—equal rights to acquire, change or retain their nationality
>—equal rights to the nationality of their children

Article 10: Equal Rights in Education

>—equal access to eduction and vocational guidance
>—the same curricula, examinations, standards for teaching and equipment
>—equal opportunity to scholarships and grants
>—equal access to continuing education, including literacy programs
>—elimination of stereotyping in education and textbooks
>—measures for reduction of female dropout rates
>—equal participation in sports and physical education
>—equal access to health and family planning information

Article 11: Employment

>—the same employment rights as men
>—free choice of profession, employment and training
>—equal remuneration, and benefits, including equal treatment as to work of equal value
>—social security
>—occupational health and safety protection
>—prohibition of dismissal on the basis of pregnancy or marital status
>—maternity leave
>—provision of social services encouraged, including child care
>—special protection against harmful work during pregnancy

Article 12: Health Care and Family Planning

—equal access to appropriate pregnancy services

Article 13: Economic and Social Benefits

—equal access to family benefits; loans and credit
—equal right to participate in recreational activities, sports, cultural life

Article 14: Rural Women

—recognition of the particular problems of rural women, the special roles they play in economic survival of families and of their unpaid work
—ensure their equal participation in development
—right to participate in development planning and implementation
—access to health care and family planning services
—right to benefit directly from social security
—right to training and education
—right to organize self-help groups and cooperatives
—right to participate in all community activities
—right to access to credit, loans, marketing facilities, appropriate technology, and equal treatment in land and agrarian reform and resettlement
—right to adequate living conditions; housing, sanitation, electricity, water, transport, and communications

Article 15: Equality Before the Law

—guarantee of same legal capacity as men; to contract, administer property, appear in court or before tribunals
—freedom of movement; right to choose residence and domicile
—contractual and other private restrictions on legal capacity of women shall be declare null and void

Article 16: Marriage and Family Law

—equal rights and responsibilities with men in marriage and family relations
—the right to freely enter into marriage and choose a spouse
—equality during marriage and at its dissolution
—the right to choose freely the number and spacing of children; access to information, education, and means to make that choice
—equal rights to guardianship and adoption of children

—the same personal rights as husband; right to choose family name, profession, or occupation
—equal rights and responsibilities regarding ownership, management, and disposition of property
—a minimum age and registration of marriage

Articles 17-22: Detail the Establishment and Function of the Committee on the Elimination of Discrimination against Women (CEDAW)

Articles 23-30: Detail the Administration of the Convention

Appendix 3

United Nations Agencies
Concerned with Women's Issues*

DAW   Division for the Advancement of Women, Vienna International Center, Center for Social, Development and Humanitarian Affairs (CSDHA), POB 500, A-1400, Vienna, Austria.

DIESA   United Nations Department of Economic and Social Affairs, United Nations, New York, NY 10017.

DPI   United Nations Department of Public Information, United Nations, New York, NY 10017.

FAO   Food and Agriculture Organization of the United Nations, Via Terme di Caracalla, 00100 Rome, Italy.

IBRD   World Bank (International Bank for Reconstruction and Development), 1818 H. Street, NW, Washington, DC 20433.

ILO   International Labour Organization, 4, route des Morillons, 1211 Geneva 22, Switzerland.

INSTRAW   International Research and Training Institute for the Advancement of Women, Apartado Postal 21747, Santo Domingo, Dominican Republic.

NGLS   United Nations Non-Governmental Liaison Service, United Nations, New York, NY 10017.

UNCHR   United Nations Centre for Human Rights, Palais des Nations, 1211 Geneva; Switzerland; and Human Rights Liaison Office, United Nations, New York, NY 10017.

UNDP   United Nations Development Programme, One United Nations Plaza, New York, NY 10017.

UNEP   United Nations Environment Programme, POB 30552, Nairobi, Kenya.

---

*Adapted from Hilka Pietila and Jeanne Vickers. Making women matter: The role of the United Nations. 1990. London: Zed Books

UNESCO	United Nations Educational, Scientific, and Cultural Organization, 7, Place de Fontenoy, 75700 Paris, France.
UNFPA	United Nations Population Fund, 220 East 42nd Street, New York, NY 10017.
UNHCR	United Nations High Commissioner for Refugees, Case Postal, CH 1211 Geneva 2 Depot, Switzerland.
UNICEF	United Nations Children's Fund, 3 United Nations Plaza, New York, NY 10017.
UNIFEM	United Nations Development Fund for Women, c/o UNDP.
WHO	World Health Organization, 20 Avenue Appia, 1211 Geneva 27, Switzerland.

Appendix 4

Nongovernmental Organizations and Institutes Concerned with Women and Global Issues

American Association of University Women, 1111 Sixteenth Street NW, Washington, DC 20036.

Associated Country Women of the World, Apt. 24, 12 Levrette, CH-1260, Nyon, Switzerland.

Bahái International Community, 866 United Nations Plaza, New York, NY 10017.

Center for Women's Global Leadership, Douglas College, Rutgers University, New Brunswick, NJ 08903.

CHANGE, 5 Central Buildings, Rye Lane, London SE 15 5DW, U.K.

Decade for Human Rights Education, 526 West 111th St., New York, NY 10025.

Grandmothers for Peace, 909 12th Street, Suite 118, Sacramento, CA 95814.

International Alliance of Women, Alemannengasse 42, 4058 Basel, Switzerland.

International Council of Women, 8 bis Montchoisis, CH-1006 Lausanne, Switzerland.

International Federation of Home Economics, 5 Avenue, de la Porte Brancion, F-75015 Paris, France.

International Federation of University Women, 30 Avenue Krieg, 1208 Geneva, Switzerland.

International Women's Rights Action Watch (IWRAW/WPPD), Humphrey Institute of Public Affairs, 301-19th Avenue, Minneapolis, MN 55415.

Jobs with Peace, 76 Summer St., Boston, MA 02110.

Mothers Embracing Nuclear Disarmament (MEND), POB 2309, La Jolla, CA 92038.

Pan Pacific and Southeast Asia Women's Association of the USA, Inc., Box 1531 Madison Square Station, New York, NY 10159.

Peace Links, 747 8th Street S.E., Washington, DC 20003.

SANE/Freeze International, 777 United Nations Plaza, New York, NY 10017.

The Women's International Peace University, 391 So. Union St., Burlington, VT 05401.

Women in International Security, Center for International Security Studies, School of Public Affiars, University of Maryland, College Park, MD 20742.

Women for a Meaningful Summit (WMS), 240 Virginia Avenue N.W., Washington, DC 20037.

Women for Mutual Security, 1 Romilia Str., GR 146 71, Castri, Greece.

Women, Public Policy, and Development Project, Humphrey Institute of Public Affairs, 301-19th Avenue, Minneapolis, MN 5514.

Women Strike for Peace (WSP), 145 South 13th Street, Philadelphia, PA 19107.

Women's Action for Nuclear Disarmament (WAND), POB 153 New Town Branch, Boston, MA 02258.

Women's Encampment for a Future of Peace and Justice, 5440 Route 96, Romulus, NY 14511.

Women's Environment and Development Organization, c/o Women USA Fund, 845 Third Avenue 15th Floor, New York, NY 10022.

Women's International Democratic Federation, Unter den Linden 13, 1080 Berlin, Germany.

Women's International Information and Communication Service, Case Postale 2471, CH-1211 Geneva 20, Switzerland.

Women's International League for Peace and Freedom (WILPF), 1213 Race Street, Philadelphia, PA 19107.

Women's Peace Initiative, 2 Lamson Place, Cambridge, MA 02139.

World Young Women's Christian Association, 37 quai Wilson, CH-1201, Geneva, Switzerland.

World Wide Network, Women in Development and Environment, 1331 H. Street N.W., Suite 903, Washington, DC 20005.

YWCA-USA, 524 9th Street NW, Washington, DC 20001.

Zonta International (ZI), 22 Avenue du Chateau, 1008 Prilly, Switzerland.

Appendix 5

Selected Bibliography on Women and Global Security Issues

There is a significant body of literature on questions related to women and peace. An excellent bibliography can be found in Berenice Carroll, "Women Take Action: Women's Direct Action for Non-Violent Social Change," *Women's Studies International Quarterly,* Vol. 12., No. 1, January 1989. Two works published in 1992, Anne Tickner's *Gender in International Relations: Feminist Perspectives on Achieving Global Security* and Spike Peterson's *Gendered States: Feminist Re-visions of International Relations* both, listed below, have very useful bibliographies. There is also a considerable number of works on women and development and a growing number on women and the environment and the human rights of women. A most extensive one on human rights is "The International Right to Non Discrimation on the Basis of Sex" by Rebecca Cook in *Yale Journal of International Law,* Vol. 14, No. 1, 1989. Works on women and development are fully annotated in *Bibliographic Guide to Studies on the Status of Women's Development & Population Trends,* UNESCO, 1983 (available from UNIPUB, 345 Park Avenue South, New York NY 10010.) The following bibliography lists but a portion of these works, focusing on those that relate to women's perspectives on and experience of the struggle for peace and feminist interpretations of other global security issues. It contains no references to the very extensive list of journal articles on these subjects; nor does it list sources on feminist theory as such.

More extensive bibliographic information is available from the Center for Women's Global Leadership and the Women, Public Policy, and Development project (see appendix 4). The works of feminist scholarship published by the State University of New York Press, the Athene series available from Teachers College Press, and the Women and World Development Series from Zed Books, Ltd., based on the JUNIC/NGO kits are recommend, especially to those seeking to construct course syllabi. So, too, are the publications of CHANGE (see appendix 4), monographs examining, global women's issues and other global issues from women's perspective and the reports available from the *International Women's Rights Action Watch* (see appendix 4).

Bartky, S. L. 1990. *Femininity and domination: Studies in the phenomenology of oppression*. New York: Routledge.

Barton, C. et al. 1991. *Women and the gulf war*. New York: Church Women United.

Beneria, L., ed. 1982. *Women and development: The sexual division of labor in rural societies*. New York: Praeger.

Bertell, R. 1985. *No immediate danger: Prognosis for a radioactive Earth*. Summertown, Tenn.: Book.

Binkin, M., and S. Bach. 1977. *Women and the military*. Washington D.C.: Brookings Institution.

Bleir, R., ed. 1986. *Feminist approaches to science*. New York: Pergamon Press.

Boserup, E. T. 1970. *Women's role in economic development*. London: Allen & Unwin.

Boulding, E. 1976. *The underside of history—a view of women through time*. Boulder, Colo.: Westview.

Boulding, E. 1977. *Women in the twentieth century*. New York: Sage.

Boulding, E. 1988. *Building a global civic culture-education for an interdependent world*. New York: Teachers College.

Branch for the Advancement of Women. 1986. *Women 2000*. Vienna: UN Center for Social Development and Humanitarian Affairs.

Brock-Utne, B. 1986. *Education for peace: A feminist perspective*. New York: Pergamon.

Brock-Utne, B. 1989. *A feminist perspective on peace and peace education*. New York: Pergamon.

Bronstein, A. 1982. *The triple struggle: Latin American peasant women*. Boston: South End Press.

Brownmiller, S. 1976. *Against our will: Men, women, and rape*. New York: Bantam.

Bulbeck, C. 1988. *One world women's movement*. London: Pluto Press.

Bunch, C., and R. Carillo. 1990. *Gender violence, a development and human rights issue*. New Brunswick, N.J.: Center for Women's Global Leadership.

Newland, K. 1982. *The sisterhood of man*. Washington D.C.: Institute for Policy Studies.

Peterson, V. S., ed. 1992. *Gendered states: Feminist re-visions of international relations theory*. Boulder: Lynne Rienner.

Pierson, R. R., ed. 1986. *Women and peace: Theoretical, historical, and practical perspectives*. London: Croom Helm.

Pietila, H., and Vickers, J. 1991. *Making women matter: The role of the United Nations*. Atlantic Highlands, N.J.: Zed Books.

Plant, J. 1989. *Healing the wounds: The promise of ecofeminism*. Philadelphia: New Society.

Report of the world conference to review and appraise the achievements of the United Nations Decade for Women: Equality, development, and peace. 1985. A/CONF. 116/28/Rev. 1. Nairobi: United Nations.

Reardon, B. 1985. *Sexism and the war system*. New York: Teachers College Press.

Rix, S. E., ed. (for Women's Research and Education Institute). 1900-91. *The American woman*. New York: Norton.

Rogers, B. 1980. *The domestication of women*. New York: Methuen.

Ruddick, S. 1989. *Maternal thinking: Toward a politics of peace*. Boston: Beacon Press.

Russell, D., ed. 1989. *Exposing nuclear fallacies*. New York: Pergamon.

Sahtouris, E. 1989. *GAIA: The human journey from chaos to cosmos*. New York: Pocket Books.

Seager, J., and A. Olson. 1986. *Women in the world: An international atlas*. New York: Simon & Shuster.

Sheridan, D., ed. 1991. *Women and peacemaking* (CSWS Review) the annual magazine of the Center for the Study of Women in Society, University of Oregon, Eugene, OR.

Shiva, V. 1988. *Staying alive: Women, ecology, and development*. London: Zed Books.

Sivard, R. L. 1976-92. *World military and social expenditures* (Annual). Washington, D.C.: World Priorities.

Sivard, R. 1985. *Women: a world survey*. Washington, D.C.: World Priorities.

Stiehm, J. ed. 1983. *Women and men's wars*. New York: Pergamon Press.

The United Nations and the world's women. 1984. Vienna: United Nations, Branch for the Advancement of Women, Center for Social Development and Humanitarian Affairs.

The United Nations and the world's women. 1986. New York: United Nations Association of the United States of America.

Tickner, J. A. 1992. *Gender in international relations: Feminist perspectials on achieving global security.* New York: Columbia University Press.

Tinker, I., and M. Bo Bransen, eds. 1976. *Women and world development.* Washington, D.C.: Overseas Development Council.

Vargas, I. 1983. *Women and violence. PRIO (Peace Research Institute Oslo) working paper 17.* Oslo: International Peace Research Institute.

Vickers, J. 1991. Women and the world economic crisis. London; Atlantic Highlands, N.J.: Zed Books.

Vickers, J. 1992. *Women and literacy.* London: Zed Books.

Waring, M. 1988. *If women counted: A new feminist economics.* New York: Haper Collins.

Woolf, V. 1966. *Three guineas.* New York: Harvest.

Wilden, A. 1987. *Man and woman, war and peace: The strategist's companion.* New York: Routledge & Kegan Paul.

World survey on the role of women in development. 1986. A/ Conf. 116/4. Rev. 1. New York: United Nations.

Notes

Chapter 1. Introduction: A Decade for Difference

1. Available from Decade Media, 118 W. 74th St., New York, N.Y. 10023.

2. A few among such men scholars are Lionel Tiger of the United States, Carlos Mallman of Argentina, and former UN Development Program officer, Erskine Childers of the United Kingdom.

3. The Nairobi Forward Looking Strategies for the Advancement of Women were produced by the UN conference held in Kenya in 1985 as the culmination of the Decade for Women.

4. The Charter of the United Nations was signed on 24, October 1945. It may be obtained from UN offices anywhere in the world.

5. The texts of all these UN documents are available from the United Nations Liaison Office on Human Rights. See appendix 3 for the address.

6. The United States as of this writing has ratified only two international instruments for the protection of human rights, the Convention on Genocide and the Convention on Civil and Political Rights.

7. Inquiries about these case studies should be addressed to the Division for the Advancement of Women, United Nations, Vienna, Austria. All of the reports and documents mentioned in this section are available from the United Nations. (See appendix 3 for addresses).

8. UN publications on the topic are part of a growing literature on this issue. International research is being conducted by Lori Heise of the World Watch Institute, Washington, D.C.

9. See, for instance, *World Military and Social Expenditures,* a report published annually, and *Women, A World Survey,* 1983. Both are published by World Priorities, Inc., Washington, D.C.

10. Karl von Clausewitz (1780-1831), the military strategist still studied as the quintessential tactician, claimed that "war is politics by other means."

11. It should be noted that the 1990 Gulf War departed from this interpretation in leaving the "enemy" government unchanged by the conflict.

12. The removal of multiple war heads from nuclear missiles was negotiated in 1992.

13. While military governments were on the wain in the 1990's, the militarization of diplomacy was not.

14. Gene Sharp, director of the Center for the Study of Non-Violent Sanctions, reported a significant increase in consultation requests in the late 1980s and early 1990s.

Chapter 2. Negative Peace: The Continuum of Violence

1. Structural violence as a concept for peace research was originally defined by Johan Galtung. In 1971 "A Structural Theory of Imperialism" reprinted in 1980 *Essays in Peace Research Volume IV* Copenhagen: Christian Eglers. pp 437-481.

2. There is some indication that this extreme differential is being reduced, particularly among urban youth, and women who have long been combatants in liberation struggles now serve as well on the frontlines of interstate warfare.

3. Among others, the works of sociologist/peace researcher Elise Boulding and historian Gerda Lerner have been particularly helpful in illuminating women's actual roles in history.

4. The Seville Statement on violence, edited with commentary by David Adams, UNESCO, Paris, 1991.

5. Lori Heise, of the World Watch Institute, Washington, D.C., is researching a book on violence against women. A longer unpublished version of the article quoted above contains an extensive bibliography on the subject.

6. Simona Shirona, an Israeli feminist, stated in a talk at Teachers College, Columbia University of New York, 7, March 1991 that during the period of Israeli incursions into Lebanon, violence against women in Israel increased. Others have corroborated this phenomenon in relation to the Gulf War.

7. The woman abused by the attorney was said to have harbored the feelings of helplessness and powerlessness that seem to paralyze such victims.

8. Among others, the National Council of Churches has undertaken a campaign to end child prostitution.

9. This crime occurred in July 1990.

Chapter 3. Positive Peace: Economic and Social Justice

1. The convention does not deal directly with domestic violence as a human rights issue.

2. Although there is no international instrument guaranteeing the right to development, it is argued that it is implied in the Convention on Economic, Social, and Cultural Rights.

3. In that the argument is made from women's perspective, it would be more appropriate to use such nonsexist language as "socially constructed" or "humanly designed."

4. Although the arms development dynamic reaching to space is no longer a competitive "race" between superpowers, there has been no halt to the possibilities of weapons in space.

5. Ruth Sivard was honored for her contributions to peace by the 1990 Pomerance Award presented by the Non-Governmental Committee on Disarmament at United Nations headquarters in New York, and by the 1991 UNESCO Prize for Peace Education.

6. *The Women's Budget* is available from the U.S. Section, Women's International League for Peace and Freedom, 1213 Race Street, Philadelphia, PA 19107.

7. Some of these "conventional weapons" border on violation of the Geneva Conventions and are complemented by other weapons of mass destruction.

8. A summary of this report, *Fact Sheet No. 21*, is available from the U.S. Department for Disarmament Affairs, United Nations, New York, NY 10021.

9. This study kit is available from the United Nation-Governmental Liaison Services. See appendix 3 for the address.

Chapter 4. Women's Roles in the Politics and Conceptualization of Peace

1. There were just such women among the Gulf Peace Team who stationed themselves at the Iraqi-Kuwaiti border before the beginning of the 1991 war in the Persian Gulf. The team was expelled by the Iraqi government. A book on these women is being written by Laurence Deonna, who won the UNESCO Prize for Peace Education for her book about Israeli and Egyptian Women, *The War and Two Voices* (see bibliography).

2. While the nuclear weapons cuts proposed in early 1992 by Presidents Bush and Yeltsin were a significant step away from the conditions of 1985, neither proposed anything as comprehensive as these "transitional measures."

3. Scilla Elworthy published *The Role of Women in Peace Movements* as Scilla McClean.

4. The 1991 session of the UN General Assembly approved a resolution on arms "transparency" that called for just such a registry of arms sales and transfers.

5. Much of this work has appeared in the *Bulletin of Peace Proposals*.

Chapter 5. Women's Visions of Peace: Images of Global Security

1. Mary Belenky, B. M. Clinchy, N. R. Goldberger, J. M. Tarule, sociologists, Carol Gilligan and Nancy Chodorow, psychologists, and Jean Baker Miller, psychiatrist, have revealed a good deal about women's thinking. Their research bases, however, are not global.

2. Imaging a World Without Weapons workshops have been developed by Elise Boulding and Warren Zeigler. These workshops are offered by the Futures Invention Laboratory. Work of a similar nature has been done for decades by the World Order Models Project.

3. The reports appear in volumes known by the names of the chairs of the independent commissions that produced them—Brandt, Palme, and Brundtland.

4. Two excellent films depicting these circumstances are *Portrait of Teeresa* from Cuba and *Raji and Kamala* from India.

5. See especially *World Military and Social Expenditures* 1984 and 1986.

6. For a consideration of alternative security systems and a proposal for common security, see Harry Hollins et al., *The Conquest of War* (Boulder: Westview, 1989).

References

Adams, D., ed. 1991. *The Seville Statement on Violence: Preparing the ground for the constructing of peace.* Paris: UNESCO. pp 16-30.

Anar, M. 1985. Boat women: Piracy's other dimension, rape and its consequences. *Refugees*, June.

Belenky, M., B. Clincly, N. Goldberger, J. Tarule. 1986. Implications for human development. *Breakthrough,* Summer, 7(4): 25-26.

Boulding, E. 1977. *Women in the twentieth century world.* New York: Sage.

Boulding, E. 1980. Women in peace research. *In women's contribution to peace movements,* ed S. Mc Lean. Paris: UNESCO.

Boulding, E. 1983. Women's concepts and skills, men's policies: The missing link for peace. Paper presented at UN experts' meeting, U.N. Branch for the Advancement of Women.

Boutros-Ghali, B. 1992. An agneda for Peace. New York: United Nations.

Bhushan, M. 1986. Women and violence. *Sangarsh.* Bangalore: Vimochna.

Brock-Utne, B. 1985. *Educating for peace: A feminist perspective.* New York: Pergamon.

Brock-Utne, B. 1989. *Feminist perspectives on peace and peace education.* New York: Pergamon.

Burns, R. 1982. Development, disarmament, and women: Some new connections. *Social Alternative* 3(1): 159-164.

Carson, R. 1962. *The Silent spring.* Boston: Houghton Mifflin.

Center for Women's Global Leadership. 1991. Violence against women violates human rights. A petition to the United Nations World Conference in Human Rights, issued from Rutgers University, December 10.

Choucri, N. 1983. Population and conflict: New dimensions of population dynamics. In *Policy development studies, no. 8,* ed. New York: United Nations Fund for Population Activities.

Cohn, C. 1987. Nuclear language and how we learned to pat the bomb. *Bulletin of the Atomic Scientists,* June, p. 17-24.

Convention on the Elimination of all forms of discrimination against Women. 1979. United Nations.

Deonna, L. 1989. The war with two voices: Testimonies by women from Egypt and Israel. Washington, D.C.: Three Continents Press.

Domestic violence against women: The hidden crime. 1989. *United Nations Focus* (U.N. Dept. of Public Information. DPI/1001), November.

Easlea, B. 1983. *Fathering the unthinkable.* London: Pluto Press.

Ehrenreich, B. and A. Fuentes. 1983. *Women in the global factory.* Boston: Southend Press.

Eisler, R. 1990. Human rights: Toward an integrated theory for action. In *The partnership way*, R. Eisler, and D. Loye. eds. San Francisco: Harper Collins.

Eisler, R. and D. Loye; eds. 1990. The partnership way. SanFrancisco: Harper Collins.

Elshtain, J. B. 1981. *Public man, private women.* Princeton, N.J.: Princeton Univeristy Press.

Elshtain, J. B. 1987. *Women and war.* New York: Basic Books.

Equal Time. 1985. 40th Anniversary Special Issue (United Nations Women's Group).

Fernand-Laurent, J. 1985. *Report on the traffic in persons and the exploitation of the prostitution of others.* New York: United Nations.

Final Document, United Nations General Assembly Special Session on Disarmament. 1978. New York: U.N. Department for Disarmament Affairs.

Final Document, International Conference on the Relationship between Disarmament and Development. 1984. New York: United Nations.

Forcey, L. R. 1987. *Mothers of sons: Toward an understanding of responsibility.* New York: Praeger.

Forcey, L. R. 1990. Feminist perspectives on mothers as peace makers: The difference vs. the equality debate and beyond. Paper presented at "Contested Terrains: Constructions of Mothering" conference, October, State University of New York, Binghamton.

French, M. 1985. *Beyond power: On women, men, and morals.* New York: Summit Books.

Galbraith, J. K. 1987. Weapons and world welfare. *Development Forum* 15(3).

Garcia, C. 1981. Androgyny and peace education. *Bulletin of Peace Proposals* 2: 163-164.

Gilligan, C. 1984. *In a different voice.* Cambridge: Harvard University Press.

Gorbachev, M. 1987. Words of welcome to the World Congress of Women. Talk presented at the World Congress of Women, June, 23, Moscow.

Heise, L. 1989. International dimensions of violence against women. *Response,* 12(1): 3-11.

Howell, B. 1978. *Women in development* (Background Paper #29). Washington, D.C.: Bread for the World.

Howell, S., and R. Willis, eds. 1989. *Societies at peace: Anthropological perspectives.* New York: Routledge.

Independent Commission on International Humanitarian Issues. 1986. *Street children: A growing urban tragedy.* London: Wildenfield & Nicholson.

INSTRAW News, No. 6. N.d. International Research and Training Institute for the Advancement of Women. Santo Domingo.

International Peace Research Association. 1983. *Conclusions of the Consultation on Women, Militarism, and Disarmament.* Gyor, Hungary: unpublished.

Inter-Parliamentary Union. 1985. *Distribution by sex of seats in parliamentary assemblies.* Geneva.

Ivey, A. 1987. President's column. *Peace and Freedom,* March.

Jobs with Peace, Campaign Report. 1991. 2(8, Winter.)

JUNIC/NGO. 1986. Anaylitic outline for development kit on women and peace. Vienna: United Nations.

Klare, M., and D. Thomas, eds. 1988. *Peace and world order studies,* 5th ed. New York: Praeger.

Kull, S. 1986. Winning the unwinnable: An interview study of the beliefs about winning a superpower war. Research paper.

Lall, B. 1987. *Security without star wars: Verifying the ban on ballistic missile defense.* New York: Council on Economic Priorities.

Levin, L. 1992. *An examination of the role of forgiveness in conflict resolution.* Ed. D. diss., Teachers College, Columbia University.

Literacy means survival. 1990. *The challenge: International literacy year news,* no. 1. Paris: UNESCO.

Making the connection: Disarmament, Development, and Economic Conversion. 1986. Geneva: International Labor Organization.

Mazrui, A. 1986. *Alternatives.*

McGinnis, J., and K. McGinnis. 1981. *Parenting for peace.* New York: Orbis.

McLean, S. ed. 1986. How nuclear weapons decisions are made. London: Macmillan.

McLean, S. E. 1988. "Women and decisions on nuclear weapons", a paper presented at the Conference on Women and Military Systems, Helsinki.

McLean, S. 1980. *The role of women in peace movements.* Paris: UNESCO.

Mische, G. 1986. The feminine and world order. *Breakthrough,* 7(4).

Mische, G., and P. Mische. 1977. *Toward a human world order.* New York: Paulist Press.

Mische, P. 1978. Women and world order. *Whole Earth Papers,* 1(8): 1-8

Mische, P. 1989. The Earth covenant: The evolution of a citizen's treaty for common ecological security. *Breakthrough,* 10(4): 31-33.

Mische, P. 1989. Ecological Security in an interdependent world. *Breakthrough,* 10(4): 7-17.

Monteville, J. 1985. A notebook on the psychology of U.S.-Soviet relationships. *Political Psychology,* June.

Myrdal, A. 1978. *The game of disarmament.* New York: Pantheon.

Nordland, E. 1991. Evaluation of a healthy society. Paper presented at the Women's World Congress for a Healthy Planet, November, Miami.

Ong, A. 1984. Industrialization and prostitution in Southeast Asia. Paper presented at a United Nations Consultation on Female Slavery.

Opotow, S. 1990. Moral exclusion and injustice: An introduction. *Journal of Social Issues,* 46(1):1-20.

Papandreou, M. 1987. Women's roles in the international arena. Speech to the conference of the World Affairs Council, April, Detroit.

Papandreou, M. 1991. A feminist foreign policy will it work. CSWS Review presented at a feminist conference. Montreal, June, and adapted for publication in annual magazine of the Center for the Study of Women in society. University of Oregon, Eugene, 6-9.

Peace is . . . no violence against women. 1986. *The Tribune.* (International Women's Tribune newsletter, New York), no. 32, 18-20.

Perez de Cuellar, J. 1987. Message of the United Nations Secretary General to the World Congress of Women: Toward 2000. Speech presented at the meetings of World Congress of Women, Moscow.

Pietila, H. 1987. Women's peace movement as an innovative component of peace movements as a whole. Paper presented at the Conference on Women and Military Systems, Helsinki.

Plotnik, M. 1991. Earth summit 1992: Setting the women's agenda. *War and Peace Digest* 1(5, December): 6.

Reardon, B. 1980. Moving toward the future. Network Newsletter Network (Washington, D.C.), January/February.

Reardon, B. 1983. A gender analysis of militarism and sexist repression: A suggested research agenda. *IPRA Newsletter,* 21(2).

Reardon, B. 1985. *Sexism and the war system.* New York: Teachers College Press.

Reardon, B. 1988. *Education for global responsibility: A guide to teacher designed curricula K-12.* New York: Teachers College Press.

Reddy, E. S. 1984. A tribute to South African women. *Pax et Libertas* (Journal of the Women's International League for Peace and Freedom, Geneva).

Roach, C. 1991. Feminist peace researchers, culture and communication. Media Development (London) 38(2).

Roberts, B. 1986. A peaceful world for women. Paper presented at the International Institute on Peace Education, July, University of Alberta, Edmonton.

Ruddick, S. 1989. *Maternal thinking: Towards a politics of peace.* Boston: Beacon Press.

Scala, A. 1988. The Colonization of our bodies: sexual voilence against women. Unpublished.

Scott, L., and B. Reardon. 1991. An ecofeminist perspective on global security. *International Journal of Humanities and Peace* (Summer).

Shelley, N. 1982. The case for a feminist contribution to peace education. Paper presented at the conference of the Australian Women's Education Coalition, October.

Shelley, N. 1983. Militarism. a conference paper.

Sivard, R. 1983. *Women: A world survey.* Washington, D.C.: World Priorities.

Sivard, R. 1977. *World military and social expenditures 1976.* Washington, D.C.: World Priorities.

Sivard, R. 1987. *World military and social expenditures 1986.* Washington, D.C.: World Priorities.

Spretnak, C. 1983. Naming the cultural forces that push us toward war. *Journal of Humanistic Psychology* (Summer).

Stephenson, C. 1985. *Alternative security systems.* Boulder: Westview Press.

Stern, M. 1991. *Security policy in transition.* Stockholm: Padriger.

Stiehm, J., ed. 1985. *Women and men's wars.* New York: Pergamon Press.

Sylvester, C. 1989. Patriarchy, Peace, and Women. In *Peace meanings, politics strategies,* ed. L. Forcey. New York: Praeger.

The consequences of inequality. 1987. International Women's News, 82: (1)1.

The crisis in education.1987. *Christian Science Monitor,* July 22, 23, 24.

The future is in their hands. 1991. *UNESCO Sources,* no.26, May.

The Nairobi forward looking strategies for the advancement of women. 1986. Vienna: United Nations Division for the Advancement of Women.

The women's budget. 1986. Philadelphia: Women's International League for Peace and Freedom, U.S. Section.

The Tribune, 1991. Newsletter 46 of the International Women's Tribune.

Thorsson, I. 1985. *Report on disarmament and development.* New York: United Nations Department for Disarmament Affairs.

Tobias, S. 1984. *A people's guide to national defense: What kind of guns are they buying for your butter.* New York: Morrow.

United Nations Decade for Disabled Persons, 1983-1992. 1991. *One in Ten* (2-3).

van Ginneker, W. 1986. Equal opportunity. In *Women at work,* no. 1. Geneva: International Labor Organization.

Weigel, K. 1990. *Women, peace and politics: The United Nations decade for women, 1975 to 1985.* University of Oregon: Honors thesis, unpublished.

Women and Aids. 1991. United Nations Department of Public Information New York DPI/996.

Women for Mutual Security. 1991a. Press release, 10 January, Baghdad.

Women for Mutual Security. 1991b. Message to the president of the United States. 14 January, Baghdad.

Women parliamentarians' statement to the United Nations Women's Decade Conference. 1985. Nairobi.

Women's issues in housing projects. 1985. UN/NGLS. New York: United Nations.

Woodward, J. Keynote address to the National Women's Conference to Prevent War, Washington, D.C. 1986.

Index

Desert Storm, 15. *See also* Persian
Gulf War
Development, economic, 100, 132,
162; and peace 144; and women,
144
Diamond, Irene, 170
DIMA (Equal Rights for the Argen-
tine Woman), 60
Disarmament, 30, 68, 124-127, 162,
166; women's perspectives on,
34; Mc Cloy-Zorin accord, 30
Double work day, 151
Dowry deaths, 50, 51

Earth Covenant, The, 160, 164
Earth-human relationship,
160-161
Earth Summit, *See* UN Conference
on Environment Development
Easlea, Brian, 47
Ecological community, vision of,
149, 160-166
Economic Conversion, 100-104, 165
Education, unequal access for
women, 87, 89-91
*Education for Peace: A Feminist
Perspective*, 137
Ehrenreich, Barbara, 106
Eisler, Riane, 74-76
Elworthy, Scilla, 32, 124
Employment, women's disadvan-
tage in, 87, 91
Enloe, Cynthia, 70
Environmental health as a security
expectation, 22-23
Environmental movement, 164
Equal Time, 116
Equality, a theme of the women's
decade, 133
Equity as a security criteria,
167-168

Feminine characteristics as approaches to peace and security,
24-27
Feminine Mystique, The, 110

Feminism, definition of, 17-18
Feminist, 20-21; security policy
questions, 166
Feminists for International Peace
and Food, 9
Five Continents Initiative (for dis-
armament), 138
Forcey, Linda, 15, 48-49, 137
Forsberg, Randall, 120, 124
*Forward Looking Strategies, See
Nairobi Forward Looking Strate-
gies*
Fragmentation of knowledge, 143
Freidan, Betty, 110
Future, the: feminine vision of, 35,
146; alternative future, 149

GABRIELA, (General Assembly
Bonding Women for Reforms,
Integrity, Leadership and Ac-
tion), 60
Game of Disarmament, The, 123,
126
Garcia, Celina, 136
Gierycz, Donota, ix
Gioseffi, Daniela, 70
Gilligan, Carol, 142
Global Education Associates, 160
Gorbechev, Mikhail, 29, 138
Goodman, Ellen, 14
Gulf War, *See* Persian Gulf War

Health care, inadequate for women,
87-88; as a criteria for the assessment of security and the environment, 88-89; women's needs for
instruction in, 90-91
Heise, Lori, 52-53
Holism as a feminine characteristic, 187
Housing, women's special need,
92-95
Human dignity as a security expectation, 23
Human needs as criteria for development and human rights, 80-87